FOUR PATTERNS

— OF —

HEALTHY PEOPLE

HOW TO GROW PAST YOUR ROOTED BEHAVIORS,
DISCOVER A DEEPER CONNECTION WITH OTHERS, AND
REACH YOUR FULL POTENTIAL IN LIFE AND BUSINESS

MATT NORMAN

Publishing services provided by 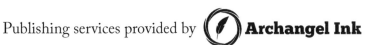 **Archangel Ink**

ISBN: 978-1-950043-12-5

This book is dedicated to Andy, Luke, and Mae. I pray that you would continue to grow into healthy people with patterns of truth and love.

ACKNOWLEDGMENTS

Thank you to my friend Peter Greer, CEO of HOPE International, for your encouragement to write this. Thank you to my dear and supportive wife, Kari, for being a truth-teller, a growth promoter, and a justice seeker. Without your truth and love, I'd have had nothing to write. Without your encouragement and belief, I'd have lost the inspiration to do it. Without your editing and thought partnership, I'd have lacked the necessary focus.

I was so fortunate to find others along this journey to carefully edit my words or my thinking. My very good friend Dan Kersten did the most developmental editing, scribbling notes on nearly every page…just because he's generous. Clara Dykstra researched examples to illustrate points and challenged my thinking. Marla Lapore made sure I came off as a decent writer and thinker as I wrote, as she has been doing for me at mattnorman.com for several years. Paul Batz and Sean McDonnell, who have teamed up on several fantastic books of their own, edited my writing and general approach to this endeavor. And, perhaps most crucially, Rob, Kristie, Erica, and the team at Archangel Ink, who helped bring this all to life.

As Steven Pressfield beautifully explains in *The War of Art*, any creative endeavor is sure to face resistance. I can't tell you how many times I sat in front of my laptop wondering how to justify the time spent on this when I could be doing something more "productive." Some of the loudest voices that countered the self-doubt were my incredible business partners Mike Scott and Amy Roberts; colleagues like Maureen Tubbs, Holly Connolly, Kevin Crone and John MacKinnon; friends Scott Rewey, Bill Bartleson, Ryan Carlson, Sean Hauenstein, and Cory Wessman; and phenomenal clients who especially encouraged this writing like Greg Breukelman, Jim Glomstad, Ryan Hagedorn, Jamie Candee and the team at Edmentum.

Thank you to my family, colleagues, and friends. Our team at Dale Carnegie, Joe Hart CEO of Dale Carnegie, and my partners around the world. Finally, thank you to my coach John March. I've grown so much through your listening and guidance.

A NOTE FROM THE AUTHOR

One of the benefits of being a consultant and coach is gaining an intimate understanding of how people and organizations operate.

As we've all seen, people typically take on jobs in areas in which they've grown, where they have experience.

An accountant had to grow her understanding of accounting standards so she now can help others to apply the same standards. A plant manager had to learn how to deal with procedural and equipment issues, and now has earned the right to direct the operations. A sales leader had to figure out how to build a book of clients and now coaches a team of salespeople trying to do the same.

But sometimes, the personal growth that's led to a current role is less obvious to the outside world.

For example, an analyst had to figure out how to deal with a demeaning boss and now leads a department with a major focus on culture and employee engagement. A lawyer got past his debilitating fear of public speaking, and today he teaches a course that helps others with their speaking.

Often our most powerful work comes out of internalized flaws, mistakes, and wounds that we've had to address.

Likewise, my motivation and capacity to help others has come primarily from the places where I've grown the most myself. My life has been an ongoing cycle of noticing what's not working, seeking out others to help me, and growing beyond the recurring themes that held me back. I'm still a work in progress. And, as you'll see in this book, I've had many helpful guides along the way.

When I look at my consulting and coaching today, I see a direct parallel between the work I do for others and the work I've done myself. That work generally falls into four "patterns" that are frequently responsible for holding people back in work and life. They are the sections that organize this book:

1. Thought patterns
2. Relationship patterns
3. Ego patterns
4. Operating patterns

By "patterns" I mean recurring themes in conflict, cognition, addictions, time allocation, and situational responses. When the patterns are well-designed, people live healthier lives—emotionally, mentally, and physically.

I hope this book, along with my stories and those of others, helps you grow beyond the recurring themes that hold you back so that you can be a healthier person.

Pattern Matching

Identifying patterns. It's one of the modern opportunities to improve productivity and performance.

Netflix does it when it suggests "other shows you might like," and Google Maps does it when it tells you to avoid a traffic slowdown.

In those cases, these systems are using artificial intelligence. But you can do it too using *human* intelligence. Take the legendary investor Warren Buffett. According to Alice Schroeder in her biography of Buffett, *Snowball*,[1] the biggest key to his investing success has been his ability to see patterns of opportunity and the compounding "snowball effect" of this knowledge. For example, in 1989, Buffett saw that Gillette had established patterns of strong brand availability and loyalty. During the 1980s, the introduction of disposable razors had hurt Gillette's sales and market share. But in that year, they introduced the Sensor Razor. Buffett saw that this would appeal to men's pattern of wanting high-tech products and that its disposable blade would set a pattern of repeat consumer purchases. As a result, his $600 million investment that year generated a $4.4 billion return through 2005, *not including annual dividends* of approximately $50 million per year.[2] That works out to about a 14% compound annual return over seventeen years. Spotting patterns can create a lot of value!

Likewise, in her book *The Mathematics of Love*,[3] Hannah Fry explains why the patterns of math and physics are powerful tools in the modern world for finding solutions to old challenges. She says, "By allowing yourself to view the world from an abstract perspective, you create a language that is uniquely able to capture and describe the patterns and mechanisms that would otherwise remain hidden."

What about your life? Have you considered that your life may largely be a set of patterns—some that bring joy, peace, and prosperity, and others that bring dysfunction, anxiety, and failure?

It's the way our human brains work.

As we think, we constantly utilize our basal ganglia, the four masses toward the back of our brains, to establish patterns. It's a survival strategy. It's our brain's way of conserving energy beneath conscious awareness. It helps us minimize use of the most resource-intensive part of our brain, the prefrontal cortex. That's where we do the tiring work of decision-making, analysis, and self-monitoring.

The subconscious part of our brain sometimes fixes into patterns of kindness, confidence, and focus, and at other times into addiction, enablement, avoidance, and distraction. Some patterns work. Others seem like they might work by offering a short-term release, escape, rush, or fix, but then…conflict, anxiety, hurt, failure.

Imagine if you could clearly see all of your patterns—the healthy and unhealthy, the productive and destructive—and grow beyond the ones that aren't working. Imagine being more mature, more authentic, clearer about your goals, calmer, more trusted, and more respected by the people you care about most.

This book is about those patterns: how to identify them, grow beyond the ones that aren't working, and enhance those that are working well. It's important to pay attention to what's working!

Practically no one is without positive traits and patterns. And it's often easiest to develop new or improved patterns by first believing in your merits. For example, maybe you've not been the best partner at home, but you're a terrific leader at work whom others trust and believe in. Perhaps you can apply the qualities from the latter to improve the former. In fact, bad patterns often develop simply by overusing or misapplying positive qualities. Furthermore, strengths can serve as a catalyst for addressing patterns that aren't working, because strengths provide confidence, energy, and even tools for improvement.

The Roots of Patterns

The first step to becoming a healthier person is understanding your patterns.

If you want to understand weather patterns, investigate climate and oceanic root causes.

If you want to understand the patterns of conflict on your team at work, look at the roots of it: analyze your narrative of the situation, how your family of origin influences your responses, whether your ego might be getting in the way, and the decisions you're making about where to spend your time. To understand this, it might be helpful to ask others who know you well enough to weigh in on your patterns. It's also the aim of this book to help you analyze the roots of your patterns.

You have a choice: you can stay stuck in your current patterns, or you can analyze and confront your patterns and grow.

Your analysis will likely reveal what psychologists refer to as "classical conditioning."[4] Beginning with the observations of Russian physiologist Pavlov and advanced by psychologist John Watson, classical conditioning tells us that our patterns develop through a history of stimulus and response. Something happens to us or within us (stimulus) and that prompts a response. If the response is rewarded, we're conditioned to respond similarly when the stimulus reappears. If the response is not rewarded or we experience pain in the response, we tend to avoid the stimulus. Culture, families, personality styles, and other factors provide the reward or pain that develop these conditioned patterns.

The amazing thing about human beings is that we can analyze our patterns and change them, despite the pain we might initially endure. Let's take a simple example. For 40 years of my life, I'd conditioned myself to eat breakfast. Various social, habitual, and physical "rewards" have patterned me to eat breakfast. The smells of breakfast, the morning calorie rush, the people around me eating…it all locked it in. Then I began to understand the health benefits of intermittent fasting, which is allowing your body a sixteen-hour rest from digesting food.[5] I decided I'd try no longer eating breakfast. At first, my body screamed at me and people thought I was strange. Then, as time passed and I faced the hunger pain and awkward reactions, I eventually started to experience the rewards of intermittent fasting. I felt healthier, more focused in the morning, and more efficient. Those rewards have now conditioned me to develop a new pattern that works better for me, one where I no longer eat breakfast.

My goal is that you will finish this book having picked up practical approaches for understanding your patterns and having grown toward your full emotional and relational potential. It's different from other self-help, motivation, or psychology books you may have read because of the depth of psychological concepts presented in an applicable format. Here you'll be presented with a series of self-assessments, worksheets, and action plans that will help you get clearer on your patterns and how to change them.

Doing the Hard Work of Growth

Our survival instincts are partially to blame for not always seeing patterns in our behavior—especially the dysfunctional ones. We humans are programmed to justify our actions and forget or ignore shortcomings that threaten our psychological well-being. In fact, it usually takes a crisis to cause us to consider what we did wrong and how we might avoid repeating our mistakes. Even then, we have a tendency to focus on fixing the symptoms, while ignoring the root causes. Worse, many of us tell ourselves we are incapable of change.

- The perfectionist continues to say "yes" to everything asked of her until she becomes so overloaded that she misses a deadline and lets her team down, yet she focuses on the failed deadline instead of why she can only feel valuable by saying yes.

- The husband continually placates his parents by manipulating situations to avoid conflict with them, shifting the conflict to his relationship with his wife, until a fight breaks out over the holidays between his wife and parents. His explanation is that his parents or wife are being difficult, but he fails to focus on his need to release the approval he still craves from his parents.

- The entrepreneur won't stop pursuing opportunities until his health or marriage break down, though his explanation centers on his wife and family not appreciating the value of his work. The real issue might be a neurotic fear of not measuring up.

- The funny colleague keeps making others laugh and feel uncomfortable until he hurts or offends someone, yet he focuses on his perception that there's too much political correctness in society. In reality, he's covering up a long-held fear that he's not smart enough.

- The person who is easily offended or triggered by others espouses "respect" and "justice" until others don't want to be around him. Rather than focusing on the sources of his own resentments, he gets angry at the insensitivity he perceives in others.

The patterns show up in slightly different ways across people, families, and organizations. Often they've been passed down through generations, corporate culture, and the general human condition.

Through my career, research, and personal experiences, I have seen people and organizations transform their unproductive patterns by addressing the underlying causes. I've coached people that others perceive to be at times distant, closed off, overly technical, insecure, insensitive, stressed, authoritative, dull, overbearing, afraid, and intimidating.

By addressing the root causes of the patterns, transformation is possible. Consider the inspiring growth of England's Prince Albert portrayed in *The King's Speech*[6] or Oprah Winfrey's transformation into a confident public figure after a childhood of insecurity due to sexual abuse and poverty.[7]

It can happen with you too.

The return-on-investment may be slow in the short term because dealing with underlying emotions can be painful. But long term, the growth is always worth it.

Others around you might not even affirm your growth unless you specifically ask them to. In fact, it may be difficult for them to see you grow because your growth may cause them discomfort or disequilibrium, prompting them to change also.

Your cognitive "hard wiring" for survival and maintaining the status quo will resist addressing the root causes of your patterns, so you need to get comfortable being uncomfortable.

For example, several years ago I began having panic attacks at work. At first, I thought it was a heart attack. They were debilitating, sidelining me at home and in my office for months. I was working hard, long hours in a stressful environment, so I focused on reducing stressors. That helped, but it didn't address the root causes. I needed to deal with my underlying need to perform and gain approval. For quite some time, that was painful work. But after gaining a much better understanding of the patterns in my thoughts and emotions and how they affected my body, I eliminated my panic attacks and substantially reduced my anxiety. I'll share later how I overcame these panic attacks.

This transformation has fueled me to study the causes and remedies to patterns in how people think, relate to others, manage their egos, and operate their lives.

I have not only researched the science behind anxiety, emotions, and relationship effectiveness, but have also applied these theories throughout our business, which coaches and advises executives on culture and talent development strategy. I've applied concepts you may have applied also, like fixed vs. growth mindset, focusing on root issues instead of symptoms, performance psychology, emotional systems theory, and humility in relationships. We will cover all of them in this book.

I will be bringing in examples from my personal life and the lives of my clients and other remarkable people to illustrate these points practically, as well as provide tools that you can use. For instance, you will learn how changing relationship patterns impacted one of the largest corporations in the world, how one of the most famous professional soccer players successfully became a stay-at-home dad, and how a men's group grew from 5 to 85 members because one member became vulnerable.

Let's dig in.

CONTENTS

CHAPTER 1

CHOOSING TO GROW

This is your last chance. After this there is no turning back. You take the blue pill, the story ends. You wake up in your bed and believe whatever you want to. You take the red pill, you stay in Wonderland, and I show you how deep the rabbit hole goes. Remember, all I'm offering is the truth. Nothing more. – Morpheus, *The Matrix*

In 2015, my wife and I agreed to bite the bullet and do marriage counseling thirteen years into our marriage. We had found ourselves in patterns of relating with one another and with our extended families in which we felt stuck. While a number of our friends had told us about breakthroughs they'd experienced doing the same, we had certain reservations. Yet we knew we'd benefit from the knowledge, experience, and counsel of a neutral third party to help us grow past our patterns of impasse. In addition, since I work in a "helping" profession as an executive coach and facilitator, receiving "help" from another professional seemed worth exploring.

The process began with a few meetings together with David, the counselor, to lay out our stories and increase our awareness of our patterns of relating, which were causing recurring misunderstanding and frustration.

After an initial few sessions to understand our situation, David pushed down deeper into our patterns of frustration. He offered me a metaphorical "red pill," like the one Morpheus offered Neo in the movie *The Matrix* to give him a new level of self-awareness and situational clarity. He wanted me to see the matrix of my life, to better understand the patterns in my thinking and behavior. These patterns had worked well enough for me. My family and early friends accepted these patterns. I didn't even think about them.

"Matt, would you talk with me alone for the next few meetings about where you can personally grow?"

He made the same offer to Kari, and we both accepted.

And into the rabbit hole we went.

Why Is Marriage Particularly Useful for Growing Up?

Psychologist and author Dr. David Schnarch calls marriage a "Human Growth Machine"[8] because it's a wrestling mat for what David Bakan describes as "the duality of human existence: isolation and communion."[9] Every human being wrestles with a longing to be accepted and a desire to be distinct. Healthy marriages (and other intimate relationships) require you to be connected while holding on to your "self." This means you must continuously learn, in the context of the relationship, to soothe your own bad feelings, pursue your own goals, and accept responsibility.

Robert Kegan puts it this way in his book *The Evolving Self*:

Evolutionarily there is a sense in which the infant (and the person throughout life) climbs out of a psychological amniotic environment. Some part of that world in which the infant is embedded nourishes his gestation and assists in delivering him to a new evolutionary balance. I call that part the embeddedness culture, that most intimate of contexts out of which we repeatedly are recreated.[10]

Think about that quote. Early in marriage, people are usually nourished by the novelty and the capacity to focus on one another. Then, as demands increase with work, children, health issues, and aging parents, the couple is usually forced out of their original amniotic environment into a new balance. From that new balance, new challenges surface, further pushing growth. Healthy people literally are continuously recalibrated...especially amidst the pressures of marriage.

While marriage creates a rich environment for growth, other intimate relationships certainly provide similar opportunities to self-confront and recreate. Working closely with colleagues, raising a child, and maintaining close friendships all provide chances to grow. It's what makes all close relationships difficult yet necessary for personal transformation.

David pointed out to me that some of my thinking and behaving was faulty, but it was so deeply ingrained in me it was impossible to see without him explaining. I had been content to think the frustration my wife experienced was because of her faulty family-of-origin patterns, which she's been open and direct about since I've known her. I honestly didn't believe that I or my family of origin had any faulty patterns in relating with people. I'm a third-generation business owner of a coaching firm that helps people relate to one another, after all! David helped me see that in protecting the idealized image I had of myself, I was rendering myself unable or unwilling to grow through old and into new patterns that would ultimately strengthen me as a husband, father, son, boss, brother, and friend, even if it came at the price of discomfort. I chose to pay the price, and the journey, though hard at times, has been worth it.

I've come to believe there will always be a distance between the present and the best version of myself. My goal is for the gap to shrink with each passing year. My hope is that more of us begin to think that way. Doesn't that represent the real richness of life's journey? The humble pursuit of intentional growth in our understanding, self-awareness, and ability to relate more deeply and meaningfully with others? Yet it's rarely our focus. We were created with vast potential to get better. Every living thing grows...and when it loses its ability or willingness to try, it no longer thrives.

As Carol Dweck says in her book *Mindset: The New Psychology of Success*: "Becoming is better than being."[11]

Her research at Stanford University revealed that human beings tend toward either a "fixed" or "growth" mindset. Fixed mindset people believe their abilities are static and, therefore, they try to *prove* themselves and the reasons for their current situation. Growth mindset people believe their abilities are dynamic, so they try to *improve* themselves. Not surprisingly, those with a growth mindset continuously improve their patterns and lead much more meaningful lives.

Fixed thoughts are very tempting. People I coach say things all the time like, "I can't do that," "I'm just so…," "She's always…," or "Our relationship will always be that way."

It's like treating a drug or alcohol addict. Most addicts are fixed in their mindset during addiction. They are so fixed they refuse to change even though they are literally killing themselves. However, with treatment that addresses the root causes of their thoughts and behaviors, addicts can recover. They literally change their neural pathways.

It's tempting to stay fixed. Growth is usually scary and uncomfortable, and it requires lots of effort. That's why human beings establish a comfort zone. Your comfort zone is the boundary between the painful and natural. And your brain is wired this way—to self-protect and avoid threats to survival.

Your amygdala, the brain's fear center, reminds you of trauma and bad past experiences, and then sends survival alerts to protect you by keeping you in the same patterns. *Be careful! Don't let something painful happen!* It resists changes or new ways of operating that seem risky. It keeps you fixed in your unhealthy patterns.

 There is nothing more difficult to carry out, nor more doubtful of success, nor more dangerous to handle, than to initiate a new order of things. – Niccolo Machiavelli

Even though your brain is wired this way, neuroscience explains that your brain can change its patterns. You don't need to be locked into limits, routines, and fears. Neuroplasticity allows your brain to reorganize itself through new connections, which manifest in new thoughts and actions.

This is great news for those of us who want to grow!

Research indicates that specific thought patterns are established based on how synapses fire along the branches of dendrites in the brain.[12] When changes are made in relationships and circumstances, the patterns permanently change. This means you can think and operate differently than perhaps you have become accustomed to after years of habit.

In other words, your comfort zone can be expanded. You were designed to grow. Your mind was made to change.

And those who grow live fuller lives and expand their capacity to impact others and the world around them.

Scott Harrison is a beautiful example of that.[13]

Scott grew up in a conservative, middle-class family in Philadelphia. At age 18, he left for New York City, where he spent the next decade working as a nightclub promoter and living a glamorous lifestyle filled with alcohol, money, drugs, and women. And then, at age 28, while he was partying on a trip in Uruguay, he had a sudden and profound realization: this was not the life he wanted to be living. In his own words, he was morally and spiritually bankrupt and knew little more than the fact that he wanted to change his patterns.

Six months later, Scott set out for a two-year journey on a hospital ship off the coast of Liberia, where he saw firsthand the devastating effects of extreme poverty and lack of access to clean water. His heart broke for the people he encountered, and he knew he would never again be able to turn his back on them.

He returned to New York in 2006 with an urgent mission to bring clean water to every person living without it. In a tiny Manhattan apartment, he brought together a small team of people and created charity:water.

Under Scott's vision and leadership, charity:water now has more than one million supporters worldwide and has funded more than 35,000 water products. Scott is the author of a *New York Times* best-selling book *Thirst: A Story of Redemption, Compassion, and a Mission to Bring Clean Water to the World*.[14] He has been recognized as one of *Fortune's* "40 under 40" and landed in the top ten of *Fast Company's* list of the Most Creative People in Business. Watch his moving story here: https://www.charitywater.org/donate/the-spring.

Tiger Woods is another example of someone who experienced profound pattern change.

Tiger grew up with high expectations for his success. Performing in front of audiences as a child and being the youngest professional golfer to win all four major golf championships (and only one of five people to do it in history!), the pressure was high. For years, many people described him as sometimes rude, arrogant, and unapproachable.

Presumably to cope with these pressures and to fuel his ego, Tiger Woods abused alcohol and had multiple sexual affairs. I'd imagine it would have been tempting at the time for him to focus on addressing his alcohol problem or his marriage problem. The reality was that Tiger needed to go deeper than that to the root causes of his problems. His identity was too closely tied to power and winning. And he likely viewed his own priorities as greater or more important than those of others.

Then he hit rock bottom. His wife left him, his body failed him in sports, and he lost…a lot.

Popular mindset about Tiger was fixed around 2015. He'd lost it. Before the scandals became public in 2009, he was the number one ranked golfer in the world. By December of 2017, he'd reached an all-time low of #1,199. He had seemingly lost everything.

Until the 2019 Masters. In what many have said is the greatest comeback story in all of sports, Tiger Woods fought to win the Masters, his first major title in eleven years. A comeback like that, in a sport so reliant on a single person's performance, is unimaginable. Even more important, though, he came back as a different person, and with a different mindset toward life and his appreciation of others. With a remade swing and aching body, he didn't win in dominant form like the days of his youth. He won with toughness, focus, and humility.

Tiger's celebration after winning and the interviews that followed revealed a different Tiger Woods. The transformed golfer was more self-effacing, more willing to appreciate others, simply more grateful.

"I was very fortunate to be given another chance to do something that I love. But more importantly, I've been able to participate in my kids' lives in a way that I couldn't for a number of years," Tiger said.

Someone close to him told *People* magazine, "He's a completely different person than he was in 2009. He was an overgrown boy back then. Now he's a man."[15]

People can get unstuck. We're all overgrown boys and girls in some ways.

I still am amazed at how much I have grown since I began meeting with David, the counselor. His influence, along with that of authors, speakers, mentors, coaches, family members, and friends, has pushed me far beyond my old patterns. If I'd had a fixed mindset, this book wouldn't exist. If Scott Harrison had had a fixed mindset, charity:water wouldn't exist. Imagine what's possible if you're willing to self-confront and grow!

PATTERN #1

HEALTHY THINKING

CHAPTER 2

THE TRUTH ABOUT YOUR THOUGHTS

You can have fears without being 'fearful.' 'Fearful' is when you let your fears make your decisions for you, so...don't let fear make your decisions for you! Having fears is normal. Being 'fearful' is dysfunctional. – **Dr. Henry Cloud,** *Boundaries for Leaders*

I was in a conference room in the Seaport District of Boston when my anxious thoughts reached a peak. Sitting at the table with my team, thoughts of insecurity and fear raced through my mind.

- *I might not have what it takes.*
- *I'm not sure if I'm good at this job.*
- *My team might not think I've earned the right to be here.*
- *People may not care what I have to say.*
- *I'm overwhelmed with everything I need to get done.*
- *What if I fail?*

Those thoughts weren't new; they had become habitual. This time they were especially intense and brought on a wave of physical reactions. I felt short of breath, my head felt heavy, my palms started sweating, it became difficult to swallow, and nervous energy swelled through my system. These physical symptoms added a layer of worry to my thoughts, all as I was trying to talk to the team.

- *Why does my body feel out of control?*
- *I can't breathe!*
- *Am I having a heart attack?*
- *I can't think!*

And before I could calm my insides down, I lost the ability to speak. The words wouldn't come out, like they were stuck in the back of my throat. The silence felt intensely awkward and paralyzing. People in the room looked curiously at me. I pretended like I needed to clear my throat. I waved off the group and walked out of the room, coughing…and mortified. In front of the bathroom mirror, I splashed water on my face and shook my head like a wet dog.

I'd had a panic attack. If you've ever had one, then you've probably experienced the same debilitating after-effect: you never want to return to the situation that produced the panic attack. The thought of reentering a conference room and going through that again terrified me like nothing I've ever experienced.

The result? I found ways to avoid speaking in any conference room at just about all costs.

Our chief operating officer had a habit of walking into people's offices and spontaneously asking them to join him in senior leadership meetings to provide an update. This was more anxiety than I could take, so I'd often close my door, turn off the light, and lie on the floor under my desk. Not only did I need to recharge my energy from the depleting effects of anxiety, I wanted it to look like no one was there. On one occasion when I was under my desk, the technology support guy came in to update my computer and screamed when he almost stepped on me.

That was my work pattern: avoiding meetings, staying out of the spotlight, and doing employee one-on-ones while walking around because movement made me less anxious.

The situation got dire. Not only was I avoiding opportunities to lead, connect, and influence, I was sometimes skipping work altogether. I was in a fixed mindset.

Anxiety Increases with Avoidance

Psychologists call this "avoidance coping," which means choosing your behavior to avoid or escape particular thoughts or feelings. The problem is that avoidance coping causes anxiety to snowball. The avoidance forms a negative reinforcement for anxiety. Each time you attempt to accomplish a goal but let fear take control and, as a result, back down, your avoidance negatively reinforces itself. The more you avoid anxious situations, the more likely you are to avoid future anxiety-inducing situations. In sum, avoidance provides short-term relief but develops a pattern of avoidance.

Here are signs that you're using avoidance to cope:

- Denying hard feelings or distress
- Escaping from uncomfortable but important situations
- Acting as though the stressor doesn't exist

The longer you avoid dealing with a stressor or tension in your thoughts or relationships, the more unmanageable the anxiety becomes. The negative reinforcement forms a continuous cycle: When you're anxious, your healthy thinking is hindered because negative cognitive biases form. You're less likely to seek support, regulate your emotions, accept yourself, engage in important activities, or challenge your faulty thinking. That cycle intensifies and has a snowball effect on your psyche.

Getting unstuck from this pattern of anxiety takes careful planning and effort, not just temporary relief.

For example, during this period of debilitating anxiety, my wife and I decided to get away for the weekend. We drove north to New Hampshire to get some rest and recovery.

We barely got there.

I remember driving up I-93 after work in rush-hour traffic with her next to me. Swirling in thoughts of anxiety, I finally became so tense I thought I could no longer breathe. Assuming I might be having a heart attack, I pulled the car over to the shoulder, got out, and walked into the ditch to calm down. No heart attack. Just more panic. I was stuck, and I knew I needed to grow.

According to the World Health Organization, more than 260 million people are living with mental health disorders.[16] A recent WHO-led study estimates that depression and anxiety disorders cost the global economy US$1 trillion each year in lost productivity. As a result, companies from Dell Technologies to Delta Air Lines now offer on-site mental health counseling for employees.[17] They realize that younger workers especially are more comfortable talking about their mental health struggles. And they're acknowledging that dysfunctional thought patterns lead to turnover and poor performance, even from people typically viewed as top performers.

It's often people you would never expect…people who are succeeding in many ways.

Rick Ankiel got drafted by the St. Louis Cardinals baseball team in 1997, right out of high school. During his first season, he broke a Single A record (previously set by his childhood idol, Dwight Gooden), going 17.3 consecutive innings without giving up a hit. The following season, he was named minor league Pitcher of the Year. Everything in baseball was going his way. Nothing to be anxious about. In fact, to challenge Ankiel, his own catcher began telling hitters what kind of pitch he was going to throw!

Ankiel's success continued when he got the call-up to the major leagues sixteen months after starting his career. In 2000, at age 20, he was in the starting rotation for the Cardinals, living the dream, doing what he loved, and doing it better than almost any human being on the planet. He was riding high—on top of the world.

Then came game one of the National League Division Series at Busch Stadium against the Atlanta Braves. Ankiel was the starting pitcher facing future Hall of Famer Greg Maddux. The entire world was tuning in to watch this 21-year-old rookie with unprecedented skill.

Everything went well until the top of the third inning, when Ankiel threw an outside "cutter" to batter Andruw Jones. It wasn't a terrible pitch, but it bounced past the Cardinals' catcher for a wild pitch. In the next three seconds, his mind flooded with anxious thoughts. *Millions and millions of people just saw me throw a wild pitch on national television,* he thought. His friends and family watching the game flashed before his eyes, along with teammates, the manager who had trusted him in game one of the playoffs, and all of the people he just knew he was letting down.[18]

Despite being ahead by a score of 6-0, he'd go on to throw four more wild pitches, issue four walks, give up four runs, and get taken out of the game before recording the third out of the inning.

Immediately following the game, he told reporters that it was a "mechanical hiccup" and that it wouldn't happen again. But the anxious thoughts were now plaguing him. *What if it happens again? What if I can't recover?*

Despite his growing panic, Ankiel was thrust back onto the mound in another playoff game and threw five wild pitches. After only two outs, he was pulled from the game.

He tried everything he could think of to avoid and cope with his anxious thoughts—superstitious routines, vodka in his water bottle…all desperation. But eventually, the only avoidance coping mechanism that made sense was to retire in 2005.

Then, only four hours after he retired, his agent, Scott Boras, called him and asked, "Are you ready to go play?"

It seemed like a crazy question, but Boras was convinced that Ankiel could get unstuck by switching positions to a spot on the field where he could have fun again. Use the strengths he did have right now, mainly his hitting. Get encouragement from the fans. Most people would have written him off, but Ankiel realized something. He had a growth mindset.

In his first game as an outfielder for the Cardinals, with two outs in the seventh inning on a two-one count, Ankiel sent the ball over the fence. Home run.

Ankiel demonstrates how susceptible people are to destructive thought patterns, and how possible it is to get unstuck. Eventually, he even returned to pitching.

Whether it's professional tennis player Mardy Fish suddenly withdrawing from the fourth round of the 2012 US Open against Roger Federer due to destructive thought patterns,[19] or Olympic swimmer Michael Phelps, who has opened up about his anxiety and depression,[20] not even the highest performers are immune to getting stuck in unhealthy patterns.

It took an extreme symptom—panic attacks—for me to come to grips with my unproductive thought patterns. But they had been there for a long time. My insecurities, fears, and worries had become habitual. Panic attacks were a dark place, but they were a wake-up call that began my journey of thinking about my thinking.

What part of your thoughts feel stuck?

Consider taking the following thought pattern self-assessment that I've developed to reveal specific ways that dysfunctional thought patterns surface for you. Everyone manifests dysfunctional thought patterns in different ways so there's no standard interpretation to how you answer these assessment items. High scores or an increase in scores may reflect unhealthy thought patterns in your life right now.

Go to www.mattnorman.com/patterns *for up-to-date printable forms and electronic assessments.*

1. Almost never 2. Rarely 3. Sometimes 4. Often 5. Regularly

#	Question	Item Score
1.	I struggle to relax.	
2.	I tend to focus on upsetting situations or events happening in my life.	
3.	I feel fearful for no reason.	
4.	I am less happy than the people around me.	
5.	When someone snaps at me, I spend a lot of time thinking about it.	
6.	No matter what I do, I can't get my mind off my problems.	
7.	I am easily alarmed, triggered, or surprised.	
8.	I experience shortness of breath or choking feelings.	
9.	I spend time wondering why I feel the way I do.	
10.	I think a lot about why I do the things I do.	
11.	I am easily irritated.	
12.	I don't express my true feelings or needs.	

#	Question	Item Score
13.	I think about all the things I have not yet accomplished.	
14.	I have trouble falling or staying asleep.	
15.	I am indecisive.	
16.	I am afraid of what awaits me in the future.	
17.	I worry what others think of me.	
18.	I can think about a problem for hours and still not feel that the issue is resolved.	
19.	I think about how unsatisfied I am with my life.	
20.	I worry a lot.	
21.	I feel tense or on edge.	
22.	I worry about my health or dying.	
23.	I have nightmares.	
24.	I self-monitor when I communicate, wondering how I'm coming across to others.	
25.	I feel I am losing control.	
26.	I never feel like I've done enough.	
27.	It pains me to disappoint people.	
28.	I worry that I'll be "found out" as being less capable than people think I am.	
29.	I think about how I compare or measure up to others.	
30.	I think about "releases" that will soothe the restless feelings inside (alcohol, tobacco, chocolate, websites).	

Increasingly, mental health issues are recognized as a common, usually treatable part of being human. Just like everyone experiences physical ailments to some degree in their life, most people will also experience psychological ailments. Yet somehow it seems obvious to talk about it and seek help when you have the flu, but shameful and private when you're feeling depressed.

Consider sharing the ways in which you responded to this assessment with people you trust so that you can talk about your thought patterns. Realize that unhealthy thought patterns tend to breed an inward focus, which leads to fear and avoidance, whereas productive thought patterns drive an outward focus on others and the world around you. This results in greater courage and willingness to care for others.

Despite the attempts that unproductive thought patterns make to protect you, they paradoxically suck the life out of you and your relationships. Talking about your thought patterns with someone you trust can be a helpful step toward changing them.

Thought Patterns Impact the People Around You

Psychology researchers Talia Zaider and Richard Heimberg from Temple University, along with Masumi Lida from Kent State University, conducted an interesting study of married couples where one partner had been diagnosed with an anxiety disorder to find out how one person's high anxiety impacts the couple as a whole.[21] Every day, the authors examined the couple's daily moods and relationship quality. What they found is fascinating yet perhaps not surprising.

Daily perceptions of relationship quality by both partners were significantly associated with the diagnosed partner's anxiety each day. Moreover, the distress levels of one partner increased during days when the other reported higher levels of anxiety, especially when one partner attempted to accommodate the other's anxiety symptoms.

One conclusion the researchers made was that "intimate relationships are a primary context in which adults express and manage personal distress." They go on to write, "The tendency to 'catch' another person's distress is referred to as *emotional contagion* and has been supported extensively in social psychology." These factors draw each partner inward, creating isolation and tension.

Why do they draw you inward? Because unproductive thought patterns are self-focused. Even if your anxiety or depression focuses on climate change or on your son who just left for college, it's still largely about your fear and how you will be impacted. As you focus on your own fears and worries, you cut yourself off from the presence and needs of others, which leads to tension and detachment.

Whether you're having panic attacks, feeling tense and overwhelmed, avoiding conflict, or experiencing any other manifestation of dysfunctional thinking, it's drawing you inward and damaging your most important relationships.

So let's dig in and look more deeply at how to start reordering the thought patterns that may keep you stuck.

CHAPTER 3

THINK ABOUT YOUR THINKING

Thoughts help define which mood we experience in a given situation. Once a mood is present, it is accompanied by additional thoughts that support and strengthen the mood. For example, angry people think about ways they have been hurt, depressed people think about how unfortunate life has become, and anxious people see danger everywhere. In fact, the stronger our moods, the more extreme our thinking is likely to be.
– Dennis Greenberger and Christine Padesky, *Mind Over Mood*

To get unstuck from unproductive patterns, many people I've coached (and I) have benefited from a workbook called *Mind Over Mood*.[22] The workbook uses a cognitive therapy approach to analyze your thought patterns. It helps you think about your thinking (referred to as metacognition).

The workbook begins by asking you to reflect on the moods that are triggering the physiological responses you're experiencing. You see, moods like anger, sadness, fear, anxiety, guilt, and shame release hormones and toxins in your body that manifest in physiological experiences like shortness of breath, headaches, fatigue, and nervousness.

During my panic attacks, I thought I had kept my moods pretty well hidden. To my co-workers, friends, and family, I seemed happy, optimistic, and confident. But that wasn't usually how my body felt. I struggled to relax. I felt shots of pain through my head and neck. I was short of breath and it was hard to swallow. My hands were often sweaty or numb, and I felt light-headed. My blood pressure was high, and I felt recurring heart palpitations.

It was also pretty clear to me what moods were persisting when my body felt this way: anxiety, overwhelm, nervousness, fear, and insecurity. These were the emotions that pulled me down.

Rather than deal with the root causes of the moods, I was managing them. I'd get massages, exercise harder, oversleep, drink alcohol, go on weekend getaways, pray, listen to music, and pour myself into work. All of those are nice things in and of themselves, but I was *using* them rather than getting totally clear and honest about what was *causing* me to feel this way.

Cognitive therapy investigates the underlying thoughts that trigger your moods. For me, the thoughts went like this:

- *What if something bad happens?*

- *I don't know if I have what it takes.*

- *What does the future hold?*

- *Am I not the top performer I thought I was?*

Those thoughts were relentless. They were accusations and threats. They came at me on my walk to work, at my desk, in meetings, and in bed. And they seemed like reasonable questions that deserved answers. So I let them come, hoping I'd sort out a clearer answer each time, not realizing they were literally hurting my body. As they came over and over again, they formed patterns, deep in my psyche.

Prior to doing this analysis, I assumed my only options for dealing with these thoughts were to ignore them, rationalize them, or simply replace them with positive thoughts. But as *Mind Over Mood* revealed, the problem with those options is that "when we feel intense moods, we're more likely to distort, discount, or disregard information that contradicts our moods and beliefs." We self-justify. It's a survival response. It's pretty difficult, over time, to debate the efficacy of your anxiety with yourself, or to just will yourself to be positive.

I learned that ignoring, replacing, or rationalizing negative thoughts is not effective. Instead, I needed to learn to accept the unproductive thoughts as part of who I am…but then deal with them appropriately.

Choose What You Pay Attention To

The great nineteenth-century psychologist William James understood that human beings normally can choose how much focus to give the thoughts that enter their minds. That choice is available because people are only capable of focusing on a finite space at any moment, which he referred to as an "attention spotlight."[23] The spotlight is literally the focus area of the mind. Outside that spotlight, little else receives conscious attention. When a threat is perceived, for instance, the attention spotlight is shifted to fight, flight, or freeze. It's a basic survival mechanism. When fight, flight, or freeze repeats itself a number of times, the spotlight holds a hypersensitive position on thoughts that reinforce the pattern. For example, when you're in the woods at night and you think you hear footsteps, your mind and body go on high alert for movement and readiness. The spotlight can literally get stuck focusing on anything that seems like more footsteps.

That same pattern develops with any unproductive recurring thoughts. You train your mind to keep the spotlight searching for footsteps.

How do you change the thoughts you spotlight, which prompt the moods that trigger the feelings in your body?

Train your mind to discern what's really true and worth spotlighting.

Teach your mind to attend to healthy thoughts rather than tension-producing ones. This can be accomplished a few ways. For example, cognitive neuroscientist Dr. Bobby Azarian uses a technique known as Cognitive Bias Modification (CBM).[24] In CBM, people are repeatedly shown a pair of images, one positive and one negative. They're asked to select the positive image over and over. After repeating this action, the selection process becomes more habitual and transferrable to other types of positive information.

Dr. Azarian explains:

Dozens of studies have confirmed the effectiveness of the regimen, and one specific study published in Clinical Psychological Science—*a journal of the Association of Psychological Science—found that playing a "gamified" CBM mobile app significantly reduced threat-bias, subjective anxiety, and observed stress reactivity, all in just a single 25–45 minute session.*

Whether you decide to download a CBM mobile app or not, the lesson is clear: Acknowledge that your mind is full of life-giving and life-draining thoughts. Then practice *choosing* the life-giving thoughts.

The key is to get curious about the thoughts. Say to yourself, "I'm having these thoughts. That's the reality of my mind right now. Where are they coming from? Are they true? And what else might be true? Which thoughts, if I pay attention to them, will lead to hope, peace, and courage?"

This requires intentional metacognition. Again, metacognition is *thinking about your thinking.* Become an observer and student of your mind. *Know thyself,* the ancient Greek aphorism suggests. When the draining thoughts come, learn to not reject or accept them. Just challenge yourself to see a fuller picture of reality (meaning the fulfilling thoughts along with the draining ones) and let the thought pass.

Let It Go and Grow

Think about your mind like a river with thoughts dropping in like leaves off trees. Green leaves represent energizing thoughts and red leaves draining ones. You can't look at all the leaves at once, so you must choose. Focus on the green leaves and let the red leaves float past. They may still be there. Don't expect them never to fall into the river. Just don't attend to them. In other words, you're not ignoring them, medicating them, or justifying them. You're acknowledging them, then consciously releasing them. If they seem too difficult to let go, try writing them down on a piece of paper and burning it. Or call a friend and tell them you're releasing them. Or gesture with your hands like you're tossing the thought aside from your head. Learn to let go.

One clear situation where draining or untrue thoughts enter the mind is during endurance competitions. In his book, *Endure: Mind, Body, and the Curiously Elastic Limits of Human Performance*, Alex Hutchinson describes the experience and mindset of people who push the boundaries of human capacity.[25] Whether the barriers are ones of pain, muscle, oxygen, heat, thirst, or fuel, these people found that the frontier of performance is in the mind. In each example, from world-record-setting underwater divers to ultra-distance runners, the mind sends warning signals to stop, to back off or slow down…for fear of survival.

But those fear warnings aren't always true. They often come far earlier than necessary for actual survival. People can push far past perceived mental limits. The mind guards your survival, but it's often much too overprotective. The limiting thoughts are real and part of who you are, but they aren't the full story. And you can only attend to part of the story. So which part will you choose to focus on? High-performance endurance competitors acknowledge the limiting thoughts but don't focus on them. They let them go.

Think about a time when you allowed perceived mental limits to detrimentally control your actions. And consider times when you've let go of those limits and pushed through.

Looking back on the time before, during, and after having several panic attacks, I notice how my thought patterns began to change. Rather than fixating on catastrophic thoughts like "What if I have a brain tumor!?" "What if the plane crashes!?" "What if I fail!?" I've learned to release those thoughts and, when appropriate, move forward despite them. I discovered that when you repeat thoughts over and over, it solidifies them. But if you hear the thought, question whether it's really true, and let it pass down the river, it quiets the thoughts. Like the result of CBM games, your patterns start to change and the negative thoughts don't keep you stuck.

I'm often reminded of when I interviewed Carolyn Smallwood, the CEO of the nonprofit Way to Grow in Minneapolis, an organization that works with parents and communities on early childhood development. "I've learned to do it *afraid*," she told me. "You get up there, and you do it, if it's the right thing to do."[26] Even when the avoidant thought patterns start coming. Even when there are red leaves filling the river, screaming YOU MIGHT FAIL, YOU MIGHT DIE, YOU MIGHT BE REJECTED, YOU MIGHT NOT BE ENOUGH…. Do it afraid. Focus on the green leaves.

When I'm speaking in front of a group of people these days, the old patterns sometimes surface, but they don't have power over me. If a thought arises like, "What if you have a panic attack!?" I take a breath, acknowledge this old pattern, open my mind to consider other more positive truths about myself, and continue speaking.

What draining or constraining thought patterns might need to change for you?

Consider these questions and thought exercises inspired by cognitive behavior therapy:

1. What recent changes have there been in my life? What have been the most stressful events for me in the past year? Three years? In childhood?

2. What physical symptoms am I having (e.g., low energy level, decreased appetite, pain, difficulty sleeping, tension, stomachaches, breathing difficulties, racing heart)?

3. What words describe my most frequent or troubling moods (e.g., sad, nervous, angry, guilty, ashamed)?

4. What behaviors are connected to my moods? At work? At home? With friends? By myself? What do I do or avoid doing?

5. When I have strong moods, what thought patterns do I have about myself? Other people? My future? What thoughts interfere with doing the things I would like to do or think I should do? What images or memories come into my mind?

Now, as you reflect on these questions, get curious about your thoughts. Which life-giving thoughts (green leaves) can you spotlight that may be truer or more consoling than the draining thoughts? Here are some unproductive thoughts that you may have, along with a question to prompt a focus on the green leaves:

Thought: I'm so overwhelmed with what I have to get done.
Question: Will this matter as much one week from now?

Thought: Am I failing?
Question: Where does my value come from?

Thought: I don't think I can do this.
Question: What challenges have I overcome in the past?

Thought: What if something happens to me or my family?
Question: What can I appreciate?

Thought: What if people think I'm not good enough?
Question: What strengths do I have?

What's another unproductive thought and question to prompt a focus on the green leaves?

Thought:

_____

_____

_____

Question:

_____

_____

_____

To understand more about your thinking, it's helpful to further investigate what might be *causing* your thought patterns. It may be helpful to better understand what values or life experiences have developed your current thought patterns. When you're clearer on what developed them, you can begin to reassess some of those values or life experiences and ultimately reduce the frequency of those thoughts.

CHAPTER 4
IDENTITY ATTACHMENTS: THE SOURCE OF YOUR UNPRODUCTIVE THOUGHTS

Getting knocked off balance can even cause you to react physically in ways that make the conversation go from difficult to impossible. Images of yourself are hardwired into your adrenal response and shaking them up can cause an unmanageable rush of anxiety or anger, or an intense desire to get away. Well-being is replaced with depression, hope with hopelessness, efficacy with fear. – Bruce Patton, Douglas Stone, and Sheila Heen, *Difficult Conversations*

What's something you value so highly that you practically *need* it to feel calm? What keeps you balanced? What's central to your identity?

Is it approval from others? Your health? Productivity? Being organized? Being right? Winning? Financial security? Happy kids? Safety? Being in control?

Each of these can be good things, even seemingly essential things. But because it's something you think you need in order to stay balanced, you might tear yourself up trying to hold on to it. As a result, it breeds resentments, fears, and behaviors that hurt others. In short, it might be the source of your unproductive thought patterns.

The fourth step of the Alcoholics Anonymous 12-Step approach to recovery is to conduct a moral inventory. You're instructed to complete a worksheet listing resentments, fears, and people you have harmed in your life. Underneath each item, you're asked to identify the root cause of your resentment, fear, or harm. Why, after all, were you so resentful, afraid, or able to hurt someone?

The purpose of this exercise is to discover the root causes or identity attachments of your unhealthy patterns. In other words, you uncover your emotional cravings and the parts of your self-image that buoy your sense of self-efficacy—the attachments that are so central that you might, literally, fall apart if you didn't have them. Resentments, fears, and harms tend to arise from a desire to protect your attachments or numb the pain of not receiving your emotional cravings.

Take some time to try doing the fourth step right now just from the events of the last month of your life. List any and all resentments, including the lady that cut you off in traffic, your wife who rebuffed you, your co-worker who got credit in a meeting, or whatever it was that frustrated you. Then list your fears. Record all the things that made you afraid, like confronting your husband, the fear of being viewed as incompetent by your peers, or speaking up in a meeting. These are just examples. After that, list the ways you harmed people. Perhaps you were harsh with your child, or maybe you gossiped about someone behind their back. Be honest about your own accountability.

Study your lists of resentments, fears, and harms over the past month. For each item you listed, what was behind it? What weren't you receiving? What part of your self-image and identity was being challenged or taken away? Often, when people complete the fourth step, they are baffled to realize how much they bury root problems and only focus on the symptoms.

Around the time of my panic attacks, many of the symptoms came as I was leading the launch of a new product for our company. I'd never launched a new product before, and this one required enormous logistical coordination. My team managed dozens of suppliers all needing to work daily on a tight schedule to produce the content and features for the product. Plus, dozens of sales and service people, along with the thousands of customers they served, were relying on our work. It was like running a newspaper or managing air traffic control.

Of course, as with any new product, there were issues. And the issues triggered calls from customers who were under high pressure by Wall Street or their other investors to make timely decisions. These calls, along with hundreds of emails every day, flooded into the sales team, creating nonstop anxiety for the company. Much of it was directed at my team.

I wondered persistently: *What if I fail at this?*

I wasn't the only one wondering that. The head of sales naturally had serious doubts about me and our team as he was dealing with his team's anxiety about getting this product running smoothly.

Even though I shared some of his doubts, I resented him at the time for his lack of confidence in me.

You see, another core value driving my self-worth was doing good work. The root issue was pride.

Now a key stakeholder in my work had questions about whether I was enough. And it knocked me off balance. I started worrying, working harder, having a drink at night, over-sleeping…all examples of symptoms. This is how most people function through life: suffer from the root cause, chase after the symptoms.

Perhaps you're overeating because of work stress. Instead of dealing with the work stress (root cause), you go on a diet to control your eating (symptom).

Another triggering event for me around this time came after I got engaged to be married. Part of the preparation was a thorough checklist of pre-wedding tasks that were recommended or required. One of them was a pre-wedding physical. I'd always been healthy and took some level of pride in my health. I exercised daily, ate well, and made other generally healthy decisions. But something came out of that physical that sent me spinning: high blood pressure.

Why would I have high blood pressure? What was wrong with me? Someone in their twenties who is in good shape and eats healthy shouldn't get high blood pressure! Or so I tried to tell myself. There must be something wrong with my heart. What if I get married and am not physically capable of providing for my wife and kids? What if my arteries harden and I die young?

I started paying close attention to my body, trying to manage the symptoms, trying to slow my heart down, eat better, meditate. I can control this, I thought. My grip on life got so tight that my mind spun webs of overblown catastrophe. When I had thought I was healthy, I'd felt in control. Now this health information had introduced questions that shook my foundational sense of self-value—all based on pride.

These pride and control factors were the root issues that contributed to my unhealthy anxious thought patterns, which were my symptoms. They represented losing (or fear of losing) things that I literally needed at the time to be OK.

Are You Attached to An Idealized Version of Yourself?

You can usually tell what you're holding on to too tightly by how connected it is to the ideal image of yourself. Consider these questions: What do you give more attention than is needed? What do you ruminate on, recycling over and over in your mind? What would you struggle to give up? Your attachment to these things might be the source of your unproductive thought patterns.

To further consider your identity attachments, think back to your most clumsy, emotional, or ugly interactions with others. It's likely that the thing (whatever it is) that you need to feel steady, which we'll call your identity attachment, was under siege in those moments. For example, you've likely had moments where strong emotions were triggered by something someone said or did to you that might not have made someone else as upset. Someone else may have just brushed it off or let it go, but for you, it represented an affront to something you hold dear about your life.

Psychologist Carl Rogers explained that life's great tension is the incongruence between your ideal self and your actual self.[27] Self-actualization, then, is the convergence of your ideal self and actual self. When there's dissonance rather than convergence, though, it can create anxiety, fear, jealousy, shame, and other difficult emotions. These emotions can drive unproductive thoughts about hopelessness, not being enough, not having value, or letting others down.

When I heard from a trusted colleague that our head of sales doubted whether I was the right person to be leading the product launch, it took my breath away, like a punch to the stomach. I'd never failed at work to this point, and I prided myself on my ability to do a good job. I was experiencing an existential crisis: my ideal self and actual self were in utter contrast.

Messages of self-doubt slowly rose to a chorus in my mind. I was protective and defensive. I became anxious in meetings, stumbling over my words and hesitating to share my ideas as I overanalyzed everything I said or did. It eventually had near-complete power over my psyche. As a result, I withdrew inward, making it harder to connect with others.

What is so central to your ideal self that, if challenged or removed, it would take your breath away? List the ten things that are most important to you in life right now, and indicate if any of them represent a gap between your ideal and actual self and are prompting unhealthy thought patterns.

The more power these identity attachments have over your psyche, the more you will likely self-protect or self-condemn with unproductive thoughts.

From Needing to Appreciating

The key to mitigating unproductive thought patterns or potential patterns is to shift from *needing* to *appreciating*. *Needing* results in attachment—we have to have it to fulfill the idealized image of ourselves. *Appreciating* results in grace and gratitude—valuing who we are and what we have. Here are six actions that will help you make that shift.

1. **Understand where you are vulnerable.** Where are you at risk of being knocked off balance by not getting what your idealized sense of self needs? Continually search your thoughts to uncover the things you think you need most. Say to yourself or someone you trust, "I am deeply programmed to desire _____ [e.g., the approval of others, to be in control, etc.]." Appreciate who you are and how you're wired.

2. **Avoid "all-or-nothing" thinking.** The primary forms of *never* or *always* thinking are denial and exaggeration. It's tempting to say or think, "I always respond to emails in a timely manner," or "I never let the house get too dirty." The reality is, no one is always or never.

Going to extremes only amplifies the identity attachment because it frames it as truer than what is actually true about you. Appreciate that you're not *always* or *never* anything.

3. **Regain your balance.** You can physically rebalance by breathing, taking a break, or doing something that brings you life. And you can mentally rebalance by moving from blame and catastrophic thinking to remembering what's true and good about you and others. Shift the spotlight to the green leaves. For me, this is a key part of my faith. It's through my faith that I have a proper perspective on who I am, the value of others, and God's story for my life. I regularly spend time alone, reminding myself that my truest identity is a beloved child of God.

4. **Resist the desire for control.** The only things you can control are your own thoughts and actions, including your reactions to others. Trying to control your circumstances or the people around you will likely leave you frustrated and cynical. Release your attempts to gain power over others, and it will lessen the power your identity attachments have over you. Appreciate your limitations and whatever comes your way.

5. **Verbalize the identity quake, when appropriate.** Talking openly about how and why you got clumsy, emotional, or ugly helps you grow through the way you react to your identity attachments. It can also be helpful for partners, colleagues, and friends to know your identity attachments. That way, when they see you clumsy, emotional, or ugly, they can respond with sensitivity. Appreciate the people around you and how each of us has a propensity toward addiction or attachment.

Everyone has identity attachments tied to the idealized image of ourselves. Many of these ideal images come from your family of origin or traumatic events of your life. These perceived needs build up throughout life as mechanisms to soothe the pain and insecurity of life.

Decide who you trust to reveal your identity attachments to, along with your strategies for appreciating rather than needing. Carl Rogers further explains that three things are required for the convergence of your ideal and actual selves: 1) an environment of genuine openness and self-disclosure, 2) acceptance (being seen with unconditional positive regard) and 3) empathy (being listened to and understood). Not having these regularly present will make you like a tree without sunlight, soil, or water. Where will you find it?

What are your identity attachments? Next, we will look at how you can confront your unproductive thoughts to get unstuck.

CHAPTER 5
FACING UNPRODUCTIVE THOUGHTS HEAD-ON

Do the thing you fear to do and keep on doing it…that is the quickest and surest way ever yet discovered to conquer fear. – Dale Carnegie

Not long after my first panic attack in a corporate conference room, my dad recommended I take the Dale Carnegie Course. This course was the same course that Warren Buffett discusses in his biography *Snowball*. It was this course that helped Buffett overcome his public speaking anxiety and apparently is the only diploma hanging on his office wall.[28] Like Buffett, it was to help me face many of my own unproductive thought patterns.

In his book *Linchpin*, Seth Godin explains the value of facing your thought patterns through self-reflection. The unhealthy thought pattern, he says, "is there, it's real, but you merely acknowledge it, you don't flatter it with rationalization or even adrenaline. It just is, and you embrace it, like a hot day at the beach (or a cold day in Minnesota). Then, an interesting thing happens. It burns itself out. The anxiety can't sustain itself forever, especially when morning comes and your house hasn't been invaded, when the speech is over and you haven't been laughed at, when the review is complete and you haven't been fired. Reality is the best reassurance of all. Over time, the cycle is broken."[29]

Each week, this course forced me to face my thought patterns and rewire the ones that weren't working.

The breakthrough came after the fifth session. I followed the instructor, Clark Merrill, out to his car.

"Clark," I pleaded. "Why am I so anxious when I'm in front of the room? It's really hard for me to do this."

Without pausing, he said, "It's not about you."

"Sure, I get that."

"Matt, it's not about you."

"Okay."

"Matt, it's not about you. Focus on the audience. Stop thinking about yourself. Face the fact that you're inwardly focused, afraid of what people will think of you. Look them in the eyes and speak to them."

The next night of the program I showed up differently. This time, when it was my turn to get up in front of the room, I faced my fears head-on, thinking about the group rather than myself. I had faced my fear by attending this course. But now, I was fully entering into my unproductive thought pattern: I was abandoning my self-protective thoughts and focusing fully on the audience.

Now, when I regularly present to boardrooms and conference rooms filled with people, I thank God for those opportunities to face my unproductive thoughts in the Dale Carnegie Course with the help of a well-trained coach.

Facing your fear and focusing on others can have profound, lasting effects.

It's why many of my close friends and colleagues started attending Alcoholics Anonymous meetings. Each of them hit rock bottom because of addictive, manipulative, and selfish thought patterns. Something in their desperation knew that if they didn't face their patterns and improve their relationships, they might lose their careers, their health, and the ones they loved the most. So they started showing up at AA meetings.

And they still go to AA meetings, even after being alcohol/drug/porn-free for years, even after relationships have healed, and even when the thought patterns seem like history. They keep going because they have realized that they need to keep facing their thought patterns with the support and accountability of others.

There's no pretense at an AA meeting. You'll find CEOs, teachers, ministers, and mechanics, rich and poor, all following a process that keeps them facing their patterns. It's a process that continuously gets them to release control of their lives and take an inventory of the fears, resentments, and harms that lead to addictive behaviors. The beauty of the process is that it's done in a group setting. Something inspirational and honest happens when you're not doing it alone. You tend to forget about yourself as you focus on and learn from others who expect you to reciprocate their honesty and accountability.

That can also happen in a group fitness class. Every day, people get on rows of stationary bikes (or at home connected to people around the world), go running in groups, and suffer through painful exercise. For many people, that's a regular confrontation of unproductive thought patterns. Most people avoid pain and seek comfort. Most people have doubts about their physical ability, rationalize exercise out of their schedule, and maintain insecurities about their body image. And yet, something profound happens when they answer the call of the alarm clock and show up for their workout buddies. It's like what my good friend Mike, who leads me and a group of friends through workouts twice a week, will sometimes say, "Boys, today is face-your-fears day."

Face your unproductive patterns and do it together.

For many of us, our potential is often hampered by too much analysis and not enough action. Facing unproductive and dysfunctional thought patterns requires showing up for the Dale Carnegie Course, the AA meeting, or the boot camp class at the gym.

It also requires saying "yes" or signing up for opportunities that will change your thought patterns.

Historian David McCullough relates that former US President Harry Truman mostly stayed home as a child, working the farm, reading, or playing the piano. His friends thought he was soft and fearful. And he would have agreed. After high school graduation, he remained on the farm and was the only president of the twentieth century who never went to college.

Shortly after high school, though, he made a fateful choice to face his careful and timid thought patterns by signing up for the army in WWI. He was shipped off to France as the head of an artillery battery. For the first time, in the midst of war, he was forced to face his insecurities and lead others.

One night in the rain, Germans dropped an artillery barrage close to his battery. Harry's troops panicked and fled. In the chaos, Truman's horse fell over on him and he was nearly crushed. Somehow the sight of his men fleeing filled him with strength. He pulled out from under the horse and called for his men to stand their ground. The men stopped fleeing, and returned, regrouped, then moved forward under Truman's leadership.

For the rest of their life, those men were loyal to Truman, their leader who refused to back down in the face of his own fear. He got unstuck and grew, which inspired his men to do the same.[30]

According to McCullough, Truman hadn't recognized his own leadership potential until that very moment. Perhaps what's most profound is that Truman put himself in a position to face his thought patterns alongside others. There are a million different decisions we can make in our lives. Choices to do nothing. Choices to avoid. And, choices to face the thought patterns that hold us back.

Keep Challenging the Patterns

Even after doing a lot of work to grow, unproductive thought patterns still linger for me. This year, for instance, I was asked to deliver the keynote address at the annual dinner for a nonprofit in our community. Every year, this event fills the local country club with neighbors, friends, and community members. So to be asked to speak to this group brought back some of those unproductive thought patterns. Rather than back down from the public speaking anxieties that resurfaced, I walked into the opportunity. Acknowledging the old thought patterns, I challenged them through self-talk and action. And I walked out the other side of the event further validating that those old destructive thought patterns don't control me anymore.

What thought patterns are you continuously facing?

In his February 2013 TEDxAustin talk, Jia Jiang explains how fear of rejection debilitated him throughout life and prevented him from pursuing his desires.[31] To deal with it, he committed himself to engaging in 100 days of rejection, where each day he did something that was sure to be rejected. His goal? Enter the fear. Face it head-on. In doing so, he would break its mystery and power over him. He's the owner of Rejection Therapy, training people to face their fears through repeated rejection It's an interesting perspective. If you want to move beyond your unproductive patterns, face them until they change.

For you, it may not be fear of rejection that keeps you stuck. Maybe it's thoughts about the unknown, fear of loss, fear of failure, fear of being known, or something else. Consider analyzing these thoughts to determine how you could enter into them to reduce their power and understand their root causes. List all of your draining thoughts: names of people, institutions, principles, or concepts that drain you.

Unproductive thought pattern:	What triggers this thought pattern?	How could you "face" those patterns?	What benefits would you expect?

Unproductive thought pattern:	What triggers this thought pattern?	How could you "face" those patterns?	What benefits would you expect?

Go to www.mattnorman.com/patterns *for up-to-date printable forms like this one along with electronic assessments.*

There you have it. Thought patterns. You can choose to pretend they're not there and just avoid or manage the symptoms. Drink more, control the people around you, eat more, watch more television, or put in more hours at work.

Or, you could face them. Understand the root causes. And do the hard work of dealing with them to experience more health and peace.

I'm not just talking about physical health and emotional/spiritual peace. I'm also referring to relational health and relational peace.

As we've discussed, our thought patterns impact the people around us as much as they impact us. In fact, our closest relationships can also be centers of our unhealthy patterns. To grow past those unproductive patterns, let's now turn our attention to relationship patterns.

PATTERN #2

HEALTHY RELATIONSHIPS

CHAPTER 6
DIFFERENTIATE YOURSELF IN RELATIONSHIPS

*I mean someone who has **clarity about his or her own life goals**, and, therefore, someone who is less likely to become lost in the anxious emotional processes swirling about. I mean someone who can be **separate while still remaining connected**, and therefore can maintain a modifying, non-anxious, and sometimes challenging presence. I mean someone who can manage his or her own reactivity to the automatic reactivity of others, and therefore be able to take stands at the risk of displeasing.* – Edwin Friedman, *A Failure of Nerve*, (bolding mine)

My parents entered the hospital room where our third child had just been born.

"It's a girl!" we said elatedly, as everyone had guessed from the way my wife carried the baby that it was a boy, joining twin brothers several years older.

With great joy they asked, "What's her name?"

"Matilda." That was the beginning of an awkward and clumsy exchange. Let's just say that name didn't make their list. It wouldn't have made ours either, years prior. But, you see, we picked it for its meaning, not its sound. Matilda means "strength in battle." We had lost six babies to miscarriages and had given up hope that we'd have another child after our twin boys. However, despite our journey of grief and loss, we delivered this beautiful child seven years later. In fact, unlike our other pregnancies, this one happened without the assistance of any fertility treatments. This child was a fighter.

I want to say that had I not been tired and sleep-deprived from the delivery (I mean, yes…my wife did most, wait, all, of the work, but, still…) I would not have been so vulnerable to desiring my parents' approval above my wife's deeply held desire. Hopefully? But their lack of initial enthusiasm unraveled me. I spent half the night awake considering the lack of popularity of that name.

I then dragged my happy, exhausted wife through an anxious reanalysis and renegotiation of our choice the following morning. Hence we changed her name to something more acceptable: Madeline.

I was so stuck in an approval pattern that rather than demonstrating solidarity with my wife, after the painful losses she'd endured over many pregnancies, I disregarded her good desire and our good choice, and convinced myself we agreed this was better.

It wasn't until months later *that I understood* my wife had never agreed. As our little girl's physical strength emerged more clearly as a six-, seven-, and eight-month-old, my wife would say, "She'll always be Matilda to me." I finally got it. So, after eight hours of paperwork, $800, and a trip to the county courthouse, she now officially is Matilda, as originally intended.

Despite my shame for compromising something as important as the name of my child, I am proud that I was able to see and accept it for what it was—an opportunity to self-confront and grow. I actually don't like talking about it, except that it gets a good laugh. Uncomfortable as it is, however, I'm glad to share it so others might benefit from it, self-confront, and grow too.

Maintaining Integrity and Healthy Relationships Sometimes Requires Conflict

In the last several chapters we discussed how our thought patterns can cause us to become avoidant. Here we look further into the ways unproductive patterns reveal themselves in relationships. Just like with thought patterns, dysfunction in relationships often stems from avoiding hard feelings and conversations.

Relationship experts often refer to conflict-avoidant stances when one person feels anxious or uncomfortable in some way.

One way of being conflict-avoidant, for instance, is to become more like someone else in hopes of gaining approval. According to Dr. Ellyn Bader, who specializes in couples therapy, many people harbor a deep fear that says, "If I express my needs and have different needs than my partner (friend, co-worker, family member), I'm going to be abandoned."[32] People often assume that, to be liked and accepted, you need to value similar things. Much of this is innate and a byproduct of thousands of years of human history, where you may get kicked out of the tribe, family, faith group, or community for having a contrary perspective or values. Being different feels risky.

Another way people avoid conflict is by not giving authentic expression to their thoughts and feelings. This fear stance says, "If I become more open and vulnerable, I'm going to get swallowed up and lose my sense of self." It's the fear that the power dynamic will shift away from you in a relationship; that admitting your flaws, talking about your emotions, or apologizing will signal weakness and loss of control. And that, by extension, might lead to rejection or loss of power.

In either avoidant pattern, according to Dr. David Schnarch, "You end up being less of a person with less of a relationship."[33]

It's all clear to me now, but it was confusing then. These were old, worn patterns. I was stuck in conflict avoidance in many of my relationships due to my desire for approval and control.

In the 1950s, American psychiatrist and professor of psychiatry at Georgetown University Murray Bowen developed a systems theory for relationships.[34] His view held that human behavior is largely a byproduct of the types of relationships one has with the people closest to them, most often their family. People seek the attention, approval, and support of and react to the needs, expectations, and disappointments of the other members of the system (family, team, close group of friends). As a result, a change in one person's functioning alters the behavior of others to the degree that the group is emotionally interdependent. In other words, your mood and behavior often change when the people you care about most change.

Problems may surface, for instance, when these people you care about get anxious about something, because the anxiety increases rapidly as it spreads to you and others in your "system." Think: one member of the team at work is highly stressed and everyone else starts feeling tense and walking on eggshells to stay clear of the anxiety.

Often one or more members of the group will find a way to step into the tension with the desire to rescue, minimize, absorb, or save others from the anxiety rather than eradicate it by addressing the real issue or letting it go. That person creates a relational triangle, amplifying the anxiety, because it's no longer just one person dealing with an issue. They are like a doctor who tries to help but eventually gets as sick as the patient.

Here's how the Bowen Center for the Study of the Family explains it:

These are the people who accommodate the most to reduce tension in others. It is a reciprocal interaction. For example, a person takes too much responsibility for the distress of others in relationship to their unrealistic expectations of him, or a person gives up too much control of his thinking and decision-making in relationship to others anxiously telling him what to do. The one who does the most accommodating literally "absorbs" system anxiety and thus is the family member most vulnerable to problems such as depression, alcoholism, affairs, or physical illness.[35]

In addition to the people in a relationship system that try to reduce the anxiety by stepping in to rescue, minimize, absorb, or save, there are also those who will attempt to reduce the anxiety by stepping out. Again, conflict avoidance can also mean running away from the problem. Some people will flee the anxiety by relocating, not attending meetings or gatherings, or simply staying out of certain conversations.

In either case, it's a dysfunctional and unhealthy pattern developed by people not able to separate their own identity and emotions from others. Psychologists refer to this as the ability to differentiate, which means staying separate (your own identity, emotions, and choices) while remaining connected (caring, loving, and present). It's knowing who you are and who you aren't. Whenever you aren't crystal clear on what defines who you are and who you aren't, parts of you will be a reflection of what you think others want you to be. And that's a dysfunctional pattern.

Affirming Who You Are Apart from the Expectations of Others

My client Adrianna is a senior research analyst running complex studies for healthcare companies. She has always seen herself as a helper. When people come to her with requests, she acts consistently with this "helper" self-image and often says yes. She also feels anxious at the thought of not being viewed this way so responds from a place of anxiety and fear of rejection.

She's decided, though, that she wants to be free to make a non-anxious choice when asked for help, one based more on her desire to serve than out of fear. So she's now reminding herself in those moments who she is and what she most values. "I am worthy regardless of how this person feels or whether their work gets done. I am valuable whether I agree to help or not." Calming her own anxiety and fear of rejection, she can then decide if she wants to help from a place of wholeness. That choice, as a result, contributes to her true identity. "I am a helper who can say 'no'" rather than "Other people expect me to be a helper so I can't say 'no.'"

Carrie, another client, struggles with a similar pattern when her brother visits her and "expects" her to pay for things. She feels anxious in the moment, thinking, "He likes that I'm generous with him, and it's going to feel awkward if I don't pay."

She's working to differentiate herself from him and these perceived expectations by reminding herself before he arrives and when they're together that she is valuable whether she pays for him or not, that she is worthy apart from what he thinks of her, even if she disappoints him. This frees her to make an authentic choice about whether to be generous. "I might choose to pay for my brother's meal because it's an act of love." That, in turn, affirms her true identity as a generous person.

We are not beholden to well-worn patterns in our relationships. Just because we grew up in a certain role, we don't have to stay in that role and should not stay in that role if it is causing dysfunction. The same is true for personal friendships, career roles, and marriages.

Do you want to clarify a distinctive identity apart from others, rather than anxiously compromising yourself and your own needs? Start making non-anxious choices to do the things that add up to you becoming the person you want to be.

Consider your closest work and personal relationships. Where do you avoid or accommodate to reduce your anxiety, rather than asserting who you really are or want to be? List below the relationships in your work and personal lives where you avoid or accommodate. For each relationship, identify how you may lack differentiation, what negative consequences surface, and what you could do to more clearly define your own self in the relationship.

| Relationship | Accommodation/Avoidance | | | | | Negative Consequences | What Could I Do to Differentiate? |
	Don't State My Needs	Don't Communicate My Feelings	Rescue Them from Their Problems	Absorb Their Anxiety	"Triangulate" Myself into Other Relationships		
Example: My Boss	Say yes to requests that are beyond my capacity	Don't communicate that I lack resources to do my work	Say "It's OK" when she arrives late	Feel tense at work whenever she's tense	Take time acting as a "counselor" to others on my team as they vent their frustrations with our boss	I'm feeling burned out due to unhealthy dynamics doing work that I love and with a boss that I like	Establish boundaries with my boss by learning to say "no" diplomatically, and proactively communicating my feelings

Go to www.mattnorman.com/patterns *for up-to-date printable forms like this one along with electronic assessments.*

One of the strongest signs that you're differentiating from others is that you're able to stay present in conversation without being as triggered or reactive, especially when you feel blamed, criticized, or hurt. The reason for this is that, when you're differentiated, you've lessened your need to get approval or affirmation from others. That said, everyone has needs, and it's very difficult to remain nonreactive and non-defensive when you feel blamed, shamed, or criticized. In the next chapter, we'll consider how to avoid reacting negatively even when the hard wiring of your brain screams at you to power up or shut down on people.

CHAPTER 7
PATTERNS OF DEFENSIVENESS IN THE FACE OF CRITICISM

Getting in line with another's feelings, rather than defending your own, puts you in a position of strength. Being defensive is the weakest posture. – David the Marriage Counselor

For most people, it's very difficult to remain differentiated, as discussed in the last chapter, when you're criticized. It's hard to hold on to yourself when you're judged or blamed by others because it can feel like the other person has power over your self-image or emotional well-being. Thoughts race through your mind like: *How could they say that about me? That's what I was* trying *to do but you wouldn't let me!*

In *The Speed of Trust*, Stephen M.R. Covey says, "We judge ourselves by our intentions and others by their behavior."[36] We compare our insides to others' outsides. Perhaps nowhere does that play out more than in our closest relationships because we depend most on them for approval and self-image.

When others show me where I'm stuck, I often don't want to listen. My intentions have solidified over years, so I know them well. I know what I am *trying* to do. I am trying to be helpful. I am trying to be loving. I am trying to be sensitive. I defend the intention, when others are impacted by the behavior. It's particularly hard to hear feedback from people I care about because they're the ones for whom I'm most *trying* to live out my intentions. When I perceive any blame or rejection, I defend myself to preserve my self-image.

The Gottman Institute, an expert source for relationship support, defines defensiveness as one of the Four Horsemen that will kill a relationship. They explain that defensiveness is a form of self-protection that furthers the cycle of blame. "You're saying, in effect, 'The problem isn't me. It's you.'"[37]

It's tempting for me to write off anyone that criticizes my behavior as judgmental, disrespectful, or unfair. Social psychologists refer to this as fundamental attribution error, which is the tendency to attribute people's behavior to their personality deficiencies.[38] In other words, when others make you upset by their criticism, your first thought might be "What a jerk" rather than considering what might legitimately have caused them to talk to you that way. On the other hand, when you act like a jerk to someone else, you tend to focus on situational factors, like how tired you are, or the reason you had to talk the way you did.

In one study, for instance, when someone did something bad, subjects blamed that person's personality 65% of the time. But when something bad happened to the subjects themselves, they blamed themselves only 44% of the time, instead pointing their finger at the situation they were in much more often.[39]

Instead of defending, according to Sheila Heen, a two-time *New York Times* best-selling author and a lecturer at Harvard Law School, healthier relationship patterns involve open discussion of each person's side of the story, with no one assuming anything about the other person.[40]

Maintaining a pattern of open discussion can be quite difficult.

When blame or criticism is being unleashed, it's important to realize that your amygdala—the part of the brain that constantly monitors threats to survival—hates criticism, judgment, and complaint. And because it's located closer to the spinal cord and central nervous system than all the rational parts of the brain, it maintains a lot of control over how you feel and react to others.

For instance, if you think that someone is criticizing, judging, or complaining about you or the things you value, your amygdala will feel threatened. In turn, your default response will be to shut down or punch back.

For example, I overheard one of my sons asking the other in a hostile tone of voice, "Why do you care so much about tennis?" This immediately elicited defensiveness, "Well, you're just jealous because I'm better at tennis than you are at baseball!" And this was the start of an incredibly unproductive argument.

The point my hostile-sounding son was *trying* to express was that he felt tennis was causing too much sacrifice for the family. But the way he brought it up caused his brother to put his guard up and start defending. All my son heard when the question came was blame and criticism. They're twelve years old and responding the way their brains are wired to respond. Threat thrown down, defense thrown back!

Especially in emotional systems at home and at work, people get easily triggered by others. It's common to feel threatened by someone attempting to get your attention or change your behavior. They might say:

- You always…

- You never…

- Why do you have to…?

When feelings or feedback get expressed this way, it's tempting for the person on the receiving end to get defensive.

To get unstuck from these patterns of tension, do your part to foster a blameless environment, which is the essence of what Dr. Marshall Rosenberg refers to as "nonviolent communication."[41] Respond in a way that makes the other person feel psychologically safe rather than attacked or threatened. Even if you *feel* like you're the one being attacked, say to yourself, "I'm feeling attacked. Rather than go into a defensive posture right now, I'm going to lower my guard and learn about the other person's side of the story." Really listen to discover what unmet need the other person is expressing to arrive at a productive set of mutual requests. That's a pattern based on concern and curiosity.

Get Unstuck by Getting Curious

The first step toward overcoming your defensiveness is to get curious about the situation and what role you have in the problem, rather than thinking you're just the victim. Acknowledge you likely play some part in the issue and be willing to accept responsibility for your part in it. This leads to more authentic and productive curiosity about the other person's side of the story, rather than falling into fundamental attribution error.

Former US President Abraham Lincoln became a master at diffusing violent communication patterns by staying curious, and it may have saved America.

Doris Kearns Goodwin points out in her book *Team of Rivals: The Political Genius of Abraham Lincoln* that Lincoln did something requiring significant mastery over his own desire to defend himself: he appointed people to his inner cabinet who criticized and competed with him.[42]

For instance, Lincoln was repeatedly opposed and insulted by the brilliant Edwin Stanton, yet he made Stanton his Secretary of War.

When Lincoln freed slaves so they could become soldiers and help the Union in the Civil War, people strongly criticized him, saying it would only prolong the war. Most Americans just wanted an end to the war, putting extreme pressure on Lincoln. Yet Lincoln stayed his course, while continuing to listen. And, despite being told he'd never win reelection, he was elected to a second term and ultimately vindicated for holding onto himself while staying open to the criticism.

"I don't like that man. I must get to know him better," Lincoln would say.

Curiosity is one of the most open postures toward another person. It's seeking to more fully know another and allow yourself to be more fully known. It is at the heart of healthy human relationships. Defensiveness does the opposite. It's guarded and walled off, prioritizing your need to be heard and vindicated. As David the marriage counselor says, it's the weakest posture.

The Strength of Curiosity

Curiosity is also essential for growth.

Harvard Business School professor Francesca Gino has conducted research suggesting that curiosity is one of the most essential traits for success. She explains:

> In my research I found that when our curiosity is triggered, we are less likely to fall prey to confirmation bias (looking for information that supports our beliefs rather than for evidence suggesting we are wrong) and to stereotyping people (making broad judgments). Curiosity has these positive effects because it leads us to generate alternatives.[43]

Curiosity in relationships means proactively listening, trying harder to understand the other person than to explain yourself, asking questions about their perceptions, and summarizing back what you've heard. It's very difficult work because it's brain-intensive and ego-threatening. It requires emotional growth because our default position is to defend and protect. The human brain is wired to survive, which is why our amygdala generates a fight-or-flight response. Truly listening to what comes back to you, not just feigning interest to patronize someone, leads to relationship growth.

My friend Megan Tamte, CEO of US retailer Evereve, works on being curious rather than defensive with her husband, Mike, who co-founded and co-leads Evereve. She explained to me:

"In relationships, I try to never get 'victimy,' pointing fingers, saying, 'You do this…' or 'You never do that.' Instead it's about saying, 'This makes me feel…. How do you see it?'"

One of Evereve's leaders recently facilitated a workshop for other leaders at the company. At the beginning of the workshop, Megan promised to do more listening than talking to allow others to participate more fully. Despite that commitment, though, she ended up jumping in and dominating the meeting when people began discussing a problem with company communication.

At that point, a teammate jumped in and said, "You weren't going to talk, and you ended up talking."

While she felt jolted by the sudden realization and was tempted to defend herself, she opened herself to the group as they explored why it's so hard for her to hold back in meetings. Ultimately, she came to the profound awareness that she needed to step back and allow others to lead, which is difficult for a founder entrepreneur.

That's breaking any patterns of defensiveness on a team!

Schnarch, whom I mentioned in the chapter 1 sidebar (page 2), was right that our close relationships (like marriage) are a human growth machine. Perhaps no one has more access to your faults and missteps than your partner, your co-workers, or your family members. They can, and often will, hold up a "mirror" to your face. See—this is what you really look like to the world! The invitation is to get unstuck and grow out of patterns that aren't working.

Will you take it?

Consider the situations where your behavior seems to most frequently frustrate others. Then, for each situation, write a curiosity question you could ask in place of defending your actions. Finally, write the outcome you'd hope for by being more curious.

Where do I frustrate others...	What curiosity question could I ask when they show frustration...	What outcome would I hope for by being curious rather than defensive...
Ex. *Showing up late.*	*How do you wish I would have communicated with you?* And even deeper... *What message does it send you when I arrive late like this?*	*The other person feels heard and understood.*

Where do I frustrate others...	What curiosity question could I ask when they show frustration...	What outcome would I hope for by being curious rather than defensive...

Go to www.mattnorman.com/patterns *for up-to-date printable forms like this one along with electronic assessments.*

We can grow our relationship patterns by taking responsibility for tension and listening with curiosity to the people closest to us. Another way is to get curious about the people who raised us and the people who raised them. Our family history may unlock more doors to getting unstuck from patterns that aren't working.

CHAPTER 8

THE ROOTS OF YOUR RELATIONSHIP PATTERNS

Our symptoms are unhealthy mechanisms that we use to keep from feeling our feelings...in dysfunctional systems, we learn early and we learn well, that to survive in the system we must pay a "small" price—we learn to deny, ignore, or escape our feelings. – John & Linda Friel

I'm guessing there's some dysfunction at your office, in your home, or in your community. The proof is on the news, in workplace surveys, and in therapy and law offices across the world. So where do these dysfunctional patterns come from? Where do any of your relationship patterns come from, for that matter?

It's possible that your patterns and the patterns around you can be traced back over many years through your family, personality, and organizational affiliations.

I grew up in a family that prioritized harmony and happiness. When conflict or hardship would arise, we'd address it and then quickly move on. "Don't go to bed angry," was a strong belief of my parents. If you spent time wallowing in negativity, they'd find a way to pull you out of it, like smiling at you until you'd laugh.

I always loved that about them. I still do. And yet as an adult, I now know that our family endured tragedies and hardships; I just didn't talk much about them. We acknowledged them on a surface-level way but we'd quickly move on. My life felt pretty safe and pretty good, pretty much all the time. On the one hand, I'm glad for that. On the other, I've realized it didn't train the muscles I'd need when life didn't feel safe, or good, because it isn't always.

We're all like fish swimming in water without thinking about the water we're in. I grew used to moving with the currents of non-confrontational Minnesota nice.

My wife's family patterns were different. She grew up on the East Coast. Her family prioritized directness and candor. Something hard or frustrating? You talked about it. Conflict with someone? Address it head-on. Don't get me wrong, they are good and loving people, but they prioritize honesty and justice in a way I had to adapt to.

Both sets of our family-of-origin's relational patterns and priorities have positives and negatives. Understanding each other's roots and historical patterns of relating allows us to be more objective about the tensions that can surface when our patterns differ/collide.

Family-of-origin patterns form the roots of your relationship patterns. Other roots can be traced to your personality tendencies.

Personality Flexibility

In the *Divergent* novel series by Veronica Roth and subsequent movies based on it, the city of Chicago has established a post-apocalyptic society segregated by personality style in order to maintain harmony.[44] The five personality style groupings are:

- Abnegation, the selfless;
- Amity, the peaceful;
- Candor, the honest;
- Dauntless, the brave; and
- Erudite, the intelligent.

In this make-believe society, you know exactly what water you swim in because your clothes and label reflect it. You take a test as a young adult to determine which "faction" aligns to your personality and you pledge your lifelong loyalty. The best way to maintain world order is to know your personality style, associate with people like you, and affirm the value of your faction. At least that was the theory.

Problems emerge, however, when sixteen-year-old Beatrice "Tris" Prior's personality test results come back inconclusive. She is a "Divergent," which means she demonstrates a mix of the styles. The excitement increases when she discovers a plot to exterminate all Divergents because they are a risk to world order. The leaders of this society wrongly thought that the best way to secure world peace was by having each personality grouping stick with the patterns of life that worked for them. Blending or working across personality styles would be too disruptive.

Many people get stuck in patterns familiar to their own style and are resistant to the preferences of other styles. Jocks hang with jocks. Musicians spend time with musicians. Type A personalities stick with other driven and achievement-oriented personalities. Building a relationship with someone from a different personality style can feel like a disruption to world order. The benefits of working through that disruption, though, are profoundly stronger, deeper, more diverse relationships that lead to better innovation, decisions, and collaboration.

To get unstuck from unproductive or one-dimensional relationship patterns, it's helpful to become more divergent. Appreciate the differences that come with other natural styles of living and relating, and try to flex and adapt to the differences.

My wife's natural style may be like Candor in Roth's post-apocalyptic society. She speaks the truth and stands up for injustice. To be more divergent, I've needed to learn to talk directly about hard things. And I've needed to learn to be more present and vocal in the face of injustice or wrongs. While it's been uncomfortable for me at times, it's made me a fuller, more productive person.

Developing more flexible personality patterns doesn't require changing who you are. What it does require is understanding how your patterns reflect your personality and becoming more agile and comfortable adapting those patterns to work well with others.

Organizationally Driven Relationship Patterns

While the roots of your relationship patterns may come from your family history or personality style, it may also be a result of the organization or community you're a part of. Players on the same team tend to develop similar patterns of relating to one another. Students at the same school establish complementary patterns. Parishioners share ways of communicating. And employees build many of their patterns based on what's modeled and rewarded at work. That's called culture.

When Satya Nadella took over as CEO of Microsoft in 2014, the company needed a turnaround. Once the gold standard for innovation in the tech world, Microsoft was quickly fading into irrelevancy. Under Nadella's leadership, Microsoft restored its performance and reputation. It has triumphed in its stock price, driving up the company's market value by more than $250 billion. What many don't know, though, is that these impressive successes can be largely attributed to an overall transformation in company culture led by Nadella.

Perhaps Nadella's most significant cultural change was transitioning the company to operate with a growth mindset. Growth mindset, again, suggests that talents and success can be generated by accepting failure as an opportunity to learn. This was a far cry from Microsoft's longstanding culture of a fixed mindset, in which talent was considered to be intrinsic and failure was not an option. In the words of one Microsoft executive, the company strived to shift from "a bunch of know-it-alls to a bunch of learn-it-alls." For instance, meetings became more open and collaborative, performance reviews were more about development than judgment, and Nadella personally modeled vulnerability by publicly admitting his mistakes.[45]

Shifts in company mindset and culture led by Nadella and senior management created a ripple effect throughout a company of 140,000 employees. Imagine that—140,000 people had built one pattern for thinking and relating and, through the leadership of one person, many (surely not all) have built new patterns for relationships at work.

If one man could change the trajectory of one of the greatest companies in the tech industry, we certainly have the capability to adapt and make changes in our own relationships.

Analyzing the roots of your relationship patterns doesn't mean rejecting your own family of origin, your personality style, or your organizational culture. It's about having a fuller appreciation and aptitude for various possible approaches to situations.

To grow in a relationship pattern might simply require additional curiosity and appreciation of another's family-of-origin experience, their personality, and their organizational culture. As we discussed in chapter 7, be curious. Topics for exploration might include money, household management, ways people show love and affection, and how people resolve conflict.

To do that, consider mapping the patterns that punctuate relationships in different parts of your life. Review your family, personality, and organizational patterns and those of others close to you. Perhaps you could grow your appreciation for other approaches, even if it initially seems to disrupt world order.

Category	Name/Relationship	How Do You Interact? (consider family, personality, and organizational affiliation influencers)	Pattern Health (1 to 10 with 10 being highly mutually healthy)
Family			
Ex. Mike/Brother-in-law		I tend to talk more and he tends to listen more. He's very accommodating (third child growing up) and I can be strong-willed (first child in my family). There's very little conflict as we are both very quick to back off if we sense the other is getting frustrated or upset. We work together so we often reflect the open communication style of our team.	9 – we have deep trust and productivity though we also need to work on having the courage to speak truth to each other and engage in productive discourse.

Category	Name/Relationship	How Do You Interact? (consider family, personality, and organizational affiliation influencers)	Pattern Health (1 to 10 with 10 being highly mutually healthy)
Work			

Category	Name/Relationship	How Do You Interact? (consider family, personality, and organizational affiliation influencers)	Pattern Health (1 to 10 with 10 being highly mutually healthy)
Personal Life			

Go to www.mattnorman.com/patterns *for up-to-date printable forms like this one along with electronic assessments.*

You may have identified relational patterns that create frustration or tension. (I'd make the case that all relationships have elements that are unhealthy or unproductive. You just have to increase your awareness or experience the stress of life to see them.) Let's conclude this chapter by focusing specifically on what dysfunctional patterns may look like.

Naming the Dysfunctional Patterns

As we discussed in chapter 6, perpetuating unhealthy relationship patterns can provide some short-term relief, but long term they create dysfunction. For instance, if a husband tends to be passive about parental discipline, the wife may need to assert herself more strongly to compensate for the father's passivity. This may create harmony between the husband and wife in the short term, but it will also lead to dysfunction, as the wife may not be able to sustain the extra responsibility, nor will the kids benefit from having only one parent assertive in discipline. The pattern becomes unhealthy because the wife and kids suffer and the husband's deficiency is enabled. Perhaps discipline was passive in the father's family growing up. Maybe he's introverted and conflict-avoidant. Perhaps no one has ever taught him how to provide healthy parental discipline. Regardless, it's creating dysfunctional tension and he needs to grow.

According to Dr. Murray Bowen's family systems theory, these are some of the most common dysfunctional patterns that derive from the roots of family origin, personality, and culture.[46] For each, list any important work or personal relationships where you see that pattern today.

Dysfunctional Pattern	Description	Relationships/Where?
Triangles	One person rescuing two others from conflict that they can or should resolve themselves, or one person rescuing another from a challenge that they can or should resolve themselves. This can also be considered over-functioning (doing something for someone that they can or should do for themselves)	
Fusion/Enmeshment	High dependence on another for acceptance, approval, and healthy functioning	
Projection	The passing of an emotional problem from one person to another—typically from parent to child—like a heightened need for attention, tendency to blame, feeling responsible for the happiness of others, lack of accountability, and impulsiveness to relieve anxiety	

Dysfunctional Pattern	Description	Relationships/Where?
Tension	Unhealthy tensions typically include: ongoing relationship conflict, dysfunction in one person that drags others down, impairment or neediness of one person, and emotional distance (usually to deal with the tension)	
Perpetuating Low Self-Definition	People associate with others that have a similar level of self-definition (clarity on preferences, values, and opinions); this perpetuates low self-definition people as they pair or hang around with people at a similar level of emotional maturity	
Emotional Cutoff	Reducing or ending emotional (not necessarily physical) contact with the group as a way of dealing with unresolved emotional issues; in some cases this may be the most appropriate response to an unhealthy system	

Other dysfunctional patterns may exist, though these six represent the primary dysfunctional patterns that can be understood and addressed. Again, addressing them may temporarily cause some relational conflict, but having the courage to address them allows you to operate with greater awareness of reality and, ideally, moves you to a new, healthier dynamic.

It's your call. Maybe you don't think it's worth it to improve the relationship that you have with your mother-in-law or colleague. Perhaps it would just be too painful, or you think your effort would be rebuffed. That's an acceptable choice; just realize that you're trading off the avoidance of discomfort in the short term for potentially a lifetime of anxiety and pain from that relationship.

By applying productive human relationship skills such as refraining from criticism, showing appreciation, being a good listener, and connecting to the desires of others, you can grow beyond these dysfunctional patterns. Even if the roots of the patterns go deep, you can do it.

One way to justify the short-term cost of growing beyond dysfunctional relationship patterns is to realize the good it will do for the relationship. It's an act of service, courage, and love to deal with what's not working in relationships. Often it's our egos that get in the way of doing this hard work. That's why we'll now turn our attention to the third type of patterns: patterns of the ego.

PATTERN #3

HEALTHY EGO

CHAPTER 9

YOUR EGO PATTERNS ITSELF ON THE EXPECTATIONS OF OTHERS

Ego (noun): A person's sense of self-esteem or self-importance. – Oxford Dictionary

We tend to let life shape us versus us shaping life. We avoid social anxiety, we buy into groupthink, and we accept many of the expectations others place on us. If we aren't deliberate about choices and planning, people around us will dictate what we value.

The best day of the summer of 2018 was the day I took my daughter to the Minnesota State Fair for the first time. The Minnesota State Fair is the culmination of summer with 320 acres of things to see and do, and it's regarded as one of the nation's top state fairs. We held hands as we walked from the car to the front entrance. She had her face elaborately painted. We sat in awe as we looked across the horizon from the top of the Ferris wheel. We took turns trying to set pull-up records with the US Marines. And she sat on my lap on a street corner, the two of us sharing a shake from the dairy barn as horses trotted past our faces. My heart swells remembering the day. What also made it great was that it was a weekday morning—one of the least-crowded times to go to the Minnesota State Fair, which can attract more than 250,000 visitors in a single weekend day.

We wouldn't have been there on that day had I not made some personal changes. You see, that summer, I decided to block time on my calendar to share weekday parenting with my wife.

My wife's default posture since having kids has been to integrate parenting into her work. I, on the other hand, operated under the assumption that my primary role was to run my business. Child care was usually an after-hours responsibility for me unless there was a specific event to attend (a school play, a teacher conference, etc.). I valued my parenting time on the weekends and evenings. But I'd generally assumed that my role, as a business owner and man, was to be fully committed to my career. Time off the business was for scheduled events like vacations, holidays, and the occasional school events. Even during those planned times off, urgent work demands needed to generally be maintained.

I'd assumed that everyone expected this of me—my family and my colleagues. Blocking time for weekday parenting terrified me. *What am I missing? What will my colleagues think? What if I'm not productive enough? How will I make the time?*

Most people play a role in life that they assume others expect of them. It may or may not be what you want, but you just don't question it, or you don't want to fail expectations. Consider the roles that you've accepted, that contribute to your self-esteem or self-importance. Have others come to expect you'll be the one to speak up about difficult topics in meetings on behalf of others? Maybe you've got it in your head that you're supposed to be the successful one in the family, so you feel stuck working in a high-paying job that sucks the life out of you. Or perhaps you really want to be a full-time parent but are afraid of what your friends will think about you when they all talk about their jobs.

The British psychologist Donald Winnicott referred to this concept of playing roles to satisfy others as the "false self." The false self, with associations to narcissism, reflects the face you portray to the world in order to be approved and accepted. The false self portrays an identity based on expectations that, somewhere along the way, form into an idealized self-image. Contrast that with what he called the "true self," which is the authentic, differentiated version of yourself.

For many people, their false self is based on how they watched their parents show up in the world, what they see peers doing, or what "shoulds" they've placed on themselves. Anything less than those expectations and you imagine that you're letting yourself and others down.

It's helpful to consider examples of people who buck expectations and define their own patterns.

For instance, when famed footballer David Beckham retired from his professional soccer career in 2013, he developed a new countercultural ego pattern: the self-proclaimed "house husband." David's wife, Victoria, had faithfully supported his career for years, and after his retirement they agreed it was her turn to commit more fully to her career. Looking after their four kids, David took on daily jobs like getting the kids ready, school drop-offs and pickups, and making dinners, while Victoria focused on her now-influential work in fashion. After years of Victoria cheering David on from the sidelines, David had become his wife's biggest cheerleader. "Victoria's success has been really incredible and, it's simple, she works really hard. She's a great mother, of course, and she looks after the boys and Harper and that's our priority and her priority, but she works really hard."

What countercultural changes to your ego patterns could you make for a more meaningful life?

This isn't just about working a flex schedule or redefining traditional gender roles. It's a decision to adjust any of the patterns that you assume are being expected of you by society and your family but aren't leading to what you value most. Consider any role patterns that you play that might need rethinking. Assess your current roles and consider which are going well and which create unnecessary anxiety, missed opportunity, or relationship tension. Try listing them here:

Role	Who Expects This of You?	How "Healthy" Is This Role?
Ex. Company leader who finds work, delivers work, and helps set direction and culture	Employees, clients, colleagues, creditors	I really enjoy and thrive in this role. At the same time, too often I carry the emotional burden of responsibility for the success of others and want to ensure everyone is happy. This can wear on me and can cause me to over-function.

Go to www.mattnorman.com/patterns *for up-to-date printable forms like this one along with electronic assessments.*

You Can Go Your Own Way

Consider the examples of others who have reset their ego patterns by defying the unhelpful expectations of society.

Monica Musonda, for instance, is breaking barriers as a female entrepreneur in Zambia. She is leading her company, Java Foods, which sources and manufactures locally to bring affordable and nutritious food to Zambian consumers. And she's doing this in an economy that is dominated by multinationals with *very* few manufacturing companies owned and operated by women. This is very countercultural and requires Monica to define her roles in very different ways from the roles that society tries to impose on her. While most of the country is following the expected pattern of outsourcing food to multinationals while women focus on domestic responsibilities, Java Foods is creating a ripple effect that will provide hundreds of jobs—from farmers to manufacturers, including many women—and will strengthen food security and the local Zambian economy.

Another example of the social impact made by someone willing to challenge society's expectations of him is Jon Pedley, a United Kingdom millionaire who built a successful telecommunications business. Pedley lived an extravagant, party-fueled life until a car accident in 2002 nearly killed him. Against all medical odds, he survived, and so began a ripple effect of change in the once self-destructive man's life. His life was transformed when he became a Christian, and in 2010 he made the decision to give away the entirety of his wealth, including his businesses and proper-ties. With these proceeds, he moved to a mud hut in Uganda and began a relief organization for orphaned children in the area. He went on to expand the program, allowing British children with a troubled past to come to Uganda to volunteer and experience some of the same heart-change that he did. Selling everything you have to live and serve amongst the poor pushes back against society's drive for money. But when asked about his decision, Pedley had few doubts—"I've never been more sure about anything in my life."[47]

While Pedley's ego patterns were interrupted by an accident, other times the interruptions happen when you surround yourself with a new set of people, even if it wasn't your choice.

Before the human rights activist became Malcolm X, the societal expectations on Malcolm Little were very low. Growing up in the foster system, he began to involve himself in criminal activity to fuel his ego through other criminals, eventually going to prison for petty larceny and breaking and entering. This trajectory is common for those who grow up in poverty through the foster system, but Malcolm broke the mold and changed his patterns. Prompting by a fellow inmate in prison transformed Little's patterns. He became aware of the teachings of the Nation of Islam.

As a symbol of his new values and pursuit of activism, he changed his last name to X to reject his slave name and launched his career of fighting for the rights of African-Americans.

These are examples of putting away the false self and changing your patterns so you can live as your true self.

How to Be Your Authentic Self Amidst Pressure to Be Someone Else

It can be really hard to be your true, authentic self in certain situations and with certain people. People with bigger jobs, bigger houses, or bigger egos can cause even the most self-assured to engage in unproductive ego patterns.

How well are you able to be your authentic self in any social environment?

The implications are significant. Be yourself and you'll experience greater peace of mind and social impact. Lose yourself and suffer from anxiety and disconnection from others.

To be more authentic, no matter the social pressures, consider the following strategies:

1. **Explore your values.** Consider what's most important to you. What concepts or pursuits most identify who you are? How would you answer this question: If people were to say anything about me, it's that I'm _____? These values likely derive from your strengths, passions, and wounds. Yes, the places where you've been hurt probably have healed into scars that define what you most value.

2. **Accept yourself and your flaws.** Once my son and I were in the car together after he'd lost a tennis match that he really wanted to win. He was tough on himself in that car ride. So we repeated this phrase to each other: *Let go and grow.* He needed to remind himself that he was enough. That he could let go of his misses and move forward.

3. **Tell the truth.** It's easy to tell small lies to impress people or minimize your flaws. *Oh yeah, I've read that book! Sure, I have an opinion on the big game! I'm great, thanks for asking!* It's hard work to act like you've done things you haven't, care about things you don't, or feel a way that's not true. Perhaps there are times when it's appropriate to go along to get along, but it usually takes something out of you.

What roles might you be playing (or not playing) as you try to maintain your false self? Consider the following assessment to determine where, and how much, you are living out your true self despite expectations of others.

1. Almost never 2. Rarely 3. Sometimes 4. Often 5. Regularly

#	Question	Item Score
1.	I intellectually rationalize decisions that I once wouldn't have made (e.g., we need the money, it's setting a good example…).	
2.	I go along to get along.	
3.	I engage in superficial politeness.	
4.	I act "as if" I have feelings in a relationship.	
5.	I carefully consider other people's expectations.	
6.	My behavior reflects societal norms.	
7.	My choices reflect expectations from parents or other authority figures.	
8.	It's difficult to be spontaneous in my words and actions.	
9.	My life is an imitation of others.	
10	My choices don't reflect my genuine preferences.	
11.	I get defensive when criticized.	
12.	I sense that I'm compensating for some insecurity or weakness.	
13.	It's difficult for me to take genuine initiative.	
14.	I'm self-conscious about what I'm doing.	
15.	I compromise what I value.	
16.	I deny or hide my feelings.	
17.	I harbor anger or resentments.	
18.	I care deeply about my mom or dad's opinion.	
19.	I'm not the source of my own action.	
20.	I crave feeling important based on the performance of my team, company, or kids.	
21.	I lack a sense of vitality.	
22.	I have a fear of being liberated to do what I really want to do.	
23.	I'm rigid or inflexible about how I think people should act.	
24.	I engage in bravado or boasting.	
25.	I'm a control freak.	
26.	I'm preoccupied by what others think.	
27.	I don't like criticism.	
28.	My choices tend to reflect those of my peers.	
29.	I act like my life is better than it is.	
30.	I don't speak up when something isn't right.	

Go to www.mattnorman.com/patterns *for up-to-date printable
forms like this one along with electronic assessments.*

If you scored,

30-60: You probably maintain a fairly low false self and probably don't play many roles out of a desire to live up to the expectations of others. Most of your choices come from a place of genuine desire and reflect your personal values though there are times, like for most people, when you may compromise your sense of self to meet the expectations of others.

61-120: You likely have a moderately false sense of self, likely due to the desire to live up to expectations others have of you. Most people are right there with you, as the desire to be accepted and approved is strong in human nature. Consider what roles you may be playing that you don't need to, or roles you need to or want to be playing that would be more in alignment with your values and preferences. Have the courage to make changes, even if you disappoint others or are met with some disapproval.

121-150: It may be quite difficult for you to be your true, authentic self, likely due to the strong pressures to be approved and accepted. This probably leads you to play several roles that you don't want to be playing or prevents you from living into roles that would truly reflect your values and preferences. Consider making strong commitments, with accountability and counsel from someone you trust, to live in greater alignment with your values and preferences, despite the risk of losing favor from others.

Ironically, the false self is most often perpetuated through an overfocus on yourself. Trying to self-protect and maintain your comfort zone leads to conformity. To get unstuck from those patterns, focus on others. The next chapter will help you reflect on where you're stuck on yourself and how that may be getting in the way.

CHAPTER 10

HUMILITY PAVES THE ROAD TO AUTHENTICITY

Humility is not thinking less of yourself; it is thinking of yourself less.
– Rick Warren, *The Purpose Driven Life*

Humility, focus on others, and recognition of your flaws form patterns of authenticity and trust. They lead to healthier relationships and greater impact on the world.

For example, I won the lottery with my first boss. She always made me feel bigger—more confident, more capable, and more valued. She was actually rather quiet and unassuming. It seemed on the surface that everyone on the team knew more than she did. But no one garnered more respect.

Years later, I worked for a different type of boss. I wondered about the source of my insecurities when I was in his presence. After all, he was nice enough, polished, talented, and smart. On the surface, he was a boss anyone would want. Yet, something was different about him compared with my first boss.

Eventually, it occurred to me that this new boss subtly reminded everyone that he was the most powerful one in the room. Whether it was name-dropping his network, not really listening when you talked, or never admitting to mistakes, his subtle plays probably made him feel bigger. The rest of us? Well, it didn't really seem to matter how we felt.

The defining quality of my first boss was evident: humility. It's what made everyone around her better. My new boss wasn't humble. He was stuck in a pattern of arrogance and pretending he had it all together.

Leadership expert Jim Collins would call my first boss a Level 5 leader. According to Collins, "Level 5 leaders display a powerful mixture of personal humility and indomitable will. They may be ambitious, but their ambition is first and foremost for the cause, for the organization and its purpose, not themselves."[48]

Consider how people at work or at home would rate your patterns of humility.

What is Humility?

Webster defines humility as "A modest or low view on one's own importance." This means not overvaluing one's own qualities at the cost of diminishing the qualities of others. A humble person avoids the spotlight and downplays their own strengths and successes. It's the person who lets their actions speak for themselves.

For a leader of others, humility takes on an added dimension related to their interactions with people who are responsible for performing tasks and achieving goals. Like the successful military leader and statesman Cincinnatus, great organizational leaders find ways to relinquish power for the good of others by not taking an arrogant view of their qualities and allowing others to express their own strengths.

When Lieutenant Dick Winters recalled the military successes of his army company, he took no credit of his own. In his best-selling memoir, *Beyond Band of Brothers*, he penned, "The cohesion that existed in the company was hardly the result of my leadership...company belonged to the men, the officers were merely the caretakers."[49] I love that. *The officers were merely the caretakers.*

Amidst all his success, Winters is most remembered by his men for his character-defining humility. As commander of his company, he would perform menial tasks alongside his soldiers and intentionally listen to those under him.

Several research studies have concluded that humble leaders are more apt to inspire great teamwork and focus everyone on organizational goals.

It's because they don't have an inflated sense of self and naturally value others. Case in point: A survey of 105 computer software and hardware firms published in the *Journal of Management* revealed that humility in CEOs led to higher-performing leadership teams, increased collaboration and cooperation, and flexibility in developing strategies.[50]

So how do you change your patterns if they lack humility, especially when your brain is wired for personal survival, drawing thoughts and desires back to yourself?

One way is to remember the priorities of your true authentic self rather than your false reflected self. It's often the case that, when you live from your false self, the self that you project to meet the world's expectations, you're much more focused on your own needs and desires. More false self, more self-focus. More true self, more capacity to focus on others. This has a compounding effect. The more you focus on yourself, the more your relationships deteriorate, prompting you to protect the ideal image of yourself in order to fuel your ego.

More True Self, More Capacity to Focus on Others

When the AIDS virus appeared on the world stage in the 1980s, it terrified everyone. The public's lack of understanding and fear of the new disease led to rampant misinformation. Most people believed that you could contract AIDS merely by touching someone who had it, and sufferers of the disease were ostracized by their communities.

But in April of 1987, Princess Diana opened a groundbreaking medical unit—the first in the UK solely devoted to the care of HIV/AIDS patients. Then she did something that shocked the world. During her visit she shook the hand of an affected patient without wearing gloves in front of global media.[51]

It is no secret that Princess Diana faced many pressures and was expected to be a lot of things to a lot of different people. When she took the risk to engage a person suffering from AIDS, she was prioritizing her true self—regardless of the outcome. As one of the world's most adored leaders, Princess Diana's single gesture of compassion helped transform society's perception of AIDS and changed the lives of thousands. More true self; more capacity to focus on others.

As a Christian, I have had the opportunity to study the life of Jesus. Regardless of what you believe about Jesus, it is hard to deny the power of his humility. Carlo Carretto writes that he chose to live "in an obscure Middle Eastern village; annihilated himself in the daily monotony of thirty years' rough, miserable work; separated himself from the society that 'counts'; and died in total anonymity."[52]

According to several documented narratives, he voluntarily made the agonizing choice to die by torture alongside criminals. And one of his last recorded acts before allowing himself to be arrested was to wash the dirty feet of his friends. His humility gave him the capacity to focus on others in profound ways. As a result, all his early followers were known to be generous, brave, charitable, and valuing of women and others marginalized by society.

That pattern has had a profound and transformative impact throughout history.

Humility Also Requires Admitting Your Mistakes

Humility also means you can admit when you're wrong or did wrong. When you live from the false self, projected to the world, it's often too painful to accept mistakes that diminish your ideal self. For instance, if you're a leader who has built his reputation on integrity and concern for others, it could prove nearly impossible to admit when you've intentionally or unintentionally wounded others in your behavior. If you're a person who prides yourself on courage and integrity, it might be excruciating to acknowledge you didn't stand up to unethical behavior.

Strong ego patterns usually lead to intolerable shame when confronted with potential flaws or mistakes.

Humility means you can acknowledge that you don't always do it right or think the right things. Openly admitting your limits and errors creates a more psychologically safe space for people to trust you and let down their own guards.

Remember to Focus on Others

You can develop the pattern of humility through constant reminders to prioritize others. Humility can be common sense but not common practice because most of life reminds us to focus on ourselves. So, to be humble, develop a habit of focusing on others.

James Clear, author of *Atomic Habits*, suggests the way to develop habits that make you more of the person you want to be is to ask:

1. How can I make it obvious?
2. How can I make it attractive?
3. How can I make it easy?
4. How can I make it satisfying?[53]

For most people, being self-effacing and others-oriented is not obvious. Society uses me-centered social media and selfies to communicate. We glorify personal achievement through academics, sports, and work. And most people's primary goal in life is to "be happy." Don't get me wrong, I use social media, take selfies, pursue achievements, and want to be happy. But the obvious center of it all is "me." What would it look like to make it obvious that you need to focus on others?

To do this, I started to put reminders in my phone. Nearly every morning, I sit at our kitchen table in the dark before anyone wakes up and I review the reminders. I pray over them. I meditate on them. They start almost every day. Here are some examples of the reminders, taken right from my phone:

- Proactively engage in the formation of our kids
- Cherish, serve, and listen to my wife
- Take initiative around the house

- Consider the needs of my extended family (and they are listed by name)
- Remember my friends and people in the community (again, listed by name)
- Be aware of the needs of colleagues and clients (listed by name)
- Support the organizations and government leaders that serve the needs of the world (listed by name)

Every day a portion of the list is reviewed to get my mind off myself and onto them.

Next, how do you make humility attractive? Perhaps one of the best ways is to surround yourself with humble people that you want to be more like. How humble are your friends, the people that you consciously or subconsciously emulate and reflect? As the saying goes, "Show me your friends, and I'll show you your future."

Then consider, how do you make humility easy? It's generally not easy when your schedule centers around yourself and your needs. Consider blocking time for service, mentoring, or just…availability. What guides your day, availability or productivity? If you're rushed, it will generally feel like an inconvenience to submit your own agenda or help someone. Remember the Biblical story of the Good Samaritan? A man is attacked by robbers and lies half-dead and naked by the side of the road. Two "religious people" walk by him (on the other side of the road), probably on their way to do "important" and religious things. Then the lowly regarded foreigner from Samaria walks by and chooses to drop what he's doing and spend his own money to care for the man. He even stays the night to make sure he's OK. It's the Samaritan that made the most significant impact on the world. Putting others before yourself like that doesn't come easy, but it's a lot harder if you're in a hurry.

Finally, how do you make humility satisfying? That's what's amazing and paradoxical about humility. Just try living with a greater focus on others, and you'll find it to be much more satisfying. Consider the joy in your relationships and the lessened anxiety as you focus more on others and less on yourself.

Build a pattern of humility. Make it obvious, make it attractive, make it easy, and make it satisfying.

One of the most important playing fields to exercise humility is in your closest and most intimate relationships. A humble others-orientation mitigates the draw toward transactional relationships that only last as long as the transaction meets the needs of the two parties. Deep, healthy relationships go beyond need fulfillment to a mutual commitment based on concern for the other person as a valuable being deserving of sacrifice and care. Let's look deeper into what that means.

CHAPTER 11

UTILITY PATTERNS IN YOUR MOST
IMPORTANT RELATIONSHIPS

Understanding singleness and marriage as callings or vocations must
inform our self-understanding and the outworking of our leadership.
– Peter Scazzero, *The Emotionally Healthy Leader*

It's easy to treat important relationships as a utility. People are "useful" when they are pleasing and satisfy needs like feeling loved, important, successful, or in control. Then, when career or personal interests become more useful than the other person, it only makes sense to move on from the relationship or disengage.

The problem with this utility pattern, which Martin Buber refers to as an "I-It" rather than "I-Thou" dynamic,[54] is that it's not an authentic human relationship and it's a dysfunctional pattern. That's because neither person in the relationship fulfills their human needs over time when one person is valued for what they *do* more than for who they *are*.

This is a common pattern, especially for busy, high-achieving people. Before a commitment like marriage, for instance, your life can be largely centered around yourself. Without a partner or dependents, you can be pretty selfish about your time and priorities. For many, when they get married, they expect their life and ambitions to continue. Sure, you can negotiate trade-offs when a child is home sick and you can't both be at work. But you still may pursue your career or other interests as hard as you can as long as the other person doesn't complain too loudly.

For the most part, these choices to focus on work or personal interests at the expense of the relationship aren't necessarily rude or inconsiderate. In fact, there may be mutual agreement that "it's going to help the family in the long run." But over time, there's a consequence to making your own needs your first consideration. Anyone who gets in the way of your needs becomes an obstacle.

It's the realization that many people come to about seven years into marriage—often referred to as "The 7-Year Itch." Perhaps the "itch" in that phrase describes the irritation married couples experience that they aren't getting all the love, esteem, success, and control they want. As a result, they want to distance themselves from the relationship, and this can lead to an affair or an addiction to something else, like work, alcohol, or porn. You see, at about the seventh year for many couples, it becomes harder to satisfy your own needs. The intimacy might not be as gratifying. Trying to have and/or raise kids can be really hard. And careers demand more and more attention. The itch raises the possibility that your relationship was too "I-It" because as soon as you stop getting the utility of the partnership, you start wondering what else might be available.

One of my good friends is a top surgeon for his specialty area of practice. It's incredibly demanding work mentally, physically, and emotionally. People come to him from long distances to improve their low chances of survival. Sadly, it's often a losing battle. Despite being among the best in the world, he regularly attends funerals for his patients. And, on top of that, any mistakes he might make would be ruthlessly scrutinized by a peer review board. The pressure and heartache come from all sides. Yet, he's expected to deal with it and move on.

For years, his pattern was to arrive home from work and pretend he was fine so that everyone would remain happy. But despite his positive intentions, stuffing his emotions actually distanced him from his wife. He'd make superficial conversation in the short time they spent together after the kids were in bed, get back on his laptop to finish up from the day, watch some television, and start the pattern again the next day. The arrangement he had with his family was a transaction. It didn't represent authentic human connection. Even though he loved them dearly, he was a utility to the family, and they were to him. For a while he and his wife survived as cordial business partners, an implicit agreement to an I-It dynamic. But eventually it led to a crisis.

Working all day, eating a meal together, and sitting in front of laptops or a television until going to bed—that's basically the definition of a roommate. It's quite different from Martin Buber's contrasting dynamic, "I-Thou," where you value each other as *people*, a genuine relationship amidst hardships, tensions, and differences.

Without continuous sacrifice and focus on the other, relationships can become utilitarian in many ways: get commitment, security, and needs fulfilled as quid pro quo. It's not just in marriage and other intimate relationships. This applies to teammates, colleagues, vendors, bosses, neighbors, and friends.

Think about the utilities that you pay for at your home. Do you know what happens when the quality of your utility provider goes down or the cost goes up? You either switch providers, or you stay with your current one and complain about it. That's how you approach your telephone, garbage removal, or electric utility.

And it's tempting to make people utilities. If you're only focused on caring for yourself, people around you become utility players—serving a need for affection, affiliation, or ambition. Trying to get to the next level in your career? Surround yourself with people that will get you there, or make you happy trying, until they aren't as useful anymore. While you and I may care about people and seem to value them highly in our lives, we're really using them on some level to get what we want.

It's probably not who you want to be, someone who uses your partner or others for your gain. It's just human nature to be self-serving in relationships. It's a pattern challenge that everyone faces.

In his song "One Step Up,"[55] Bruce Springsteen says of his troubled marriage that it often felt like moving one step up and two steps back because he would slip off track from being the person he wanted to be. Perhaps you've felt that way at times too.

I've talked to countless people who would describe their relationship trajectories in similar ways. Not bad, sometimes great, sometimes really hard, almost always not quite what they wanted it to be. The only solution is to change the pattern and place your important relationships above your personal ambitions, letting this inform your choices about where to spend your time and what to sacrifice.

This requires making a commitment to *serving* over other worldly pursuits. It means cherishing and caring for the people close to you every day the way you might for a child. This doesn't mean doing things for them that they can do for themselves or rescuing them from the hard parts of life that they need to face. It simply means an all-out willingness to put the good of the other above your personal need for importance, success, and control. It means ensuring their needs are addressed and that they know they are loved, even before fulfilling the demands and desires of life like work commitments and childcare responsibilities.

Through my work with countless leaders at varying levels across different cultures, it's the only way I've found to thrive in your family, career, and personal interests. Develop a pattern that puts your most important relationships before your personal ambitions and you'll experience much greater joy and energy over time.

True Commitment Requires Sacrifice

A prevalent yet quickly dismissed problem in intimate relationships is workaholism, especially in America. Psychotherapist and professor emeritus at the University of North Carolina at Charlotte Dr. Bryan Robinson has dedicated much of his work to research and advocacy about the dangers of workaholism. He refers to it as "the best-dressed problem of the twenty-first century."[56] It's no surprise that in a society driven largely by status and success, work addiction is normalized—even celebrated—but it comes at a high price. At its best, it leads to burnout and exhaustion. At its worst, workaholism can be a silent destroyer of marriages and families: mutual support disappears amongst a couple, and children can feel disconnected from their distant parent.

Dr. Robinson is no stranger to this phenomenon. His workaholism drove him to the brink in 1983, when his life partner left him out of frustration over his habits. Robinson was doing everything right by society's standards—making major strides in his career through his academic contributions. Inside, though, he felt empty and alone. It wasn't until he was confronted later that year about his obsession to work that he was able to piece together why his relationships were failing.

He reconnected with his partner, went to therapy, and sought help for his addiction. He has continued to make incredible academic contributions throughout his lifetime, including his highly regarded book *Chained to the Desk: A Guidebook for Workaholics, Their Partners and Children, and the Clinicians Who Treat Them*, but now work is not his number one priority. Referring to himself as a "recovering workaholic," he makes the choice to invest in moments and relationships—and he and his family are better for it.

Andy Stanley understands this tension very well.[57] His father and mother, Charles and Anna Stanley, divorced after 40 years, perhaps as a result of Charles's larger-than-life visibility as a prominent Baptist minister who led an enormous church in Atlanta and founded a worldwide evangelism TV network.

When Andy founded his own organization, North Point Community Church, he set boundaries. He asked his wife, who was raising three kids in diapers, what the hardest time of the day was for her. No doubt about it, came the response: 4:30 p.m. The kids are tired, she's tired, and dinner needs to be made. So, despite having just founded a rapidly growing organization, he told his young staff that he'd be leaving the office before 4:30 every day, regardless of what was going on.

This boundary required enormous humility because, as Andy says, his prevailing mindset was, "If I don't _____, it won't _____." In other words, he thought his importance to the organization required him to be present and active if progress were to be made. He had to let go of that sense of self-importance, along with the worry that his organization may not be as successful as he'd like it to be due to his sacrifice to be home early every day. He decided, as painful as it might be at times for his ego, to lead his organization out of a strong marriage rather than in spite of his marriage commitment.

If you need to work late checking email instead of connecting with your partner, fine. But don't make it a habit or you'll pay for it later.

If your schedule is packed with activities, make sure some time is scheduled for the people who will be by your side in your life's final hours. Everyone and everything else should take second priority. When you do this, others will notice that you show up differently in the world because of your faithful commitment to what matters most to you.

These sacrifices require the faith that it will lead to a stronger relationship, and a strong relationship will make you a more impactful, more joyful, and more sustainable leader.

Let's face it. Most people slip into utilitarian, transactional patterns without even knowing it. So many couples get married with a lot in common, but completely lose touch and become strangers by the time their kids go to college. Why? Because over time, we are drawn to pursue our own needs, preferences, and ambitions rather than taking the uncomfortable road of authentic sacrifice.

What career or personal sacrifice could you make to set a pattern that truly prioritizes your most important relationships? It's a very difficult question to answer because it's not natural to allow others to move in front of you in line or to do things that are painful to your ego. Your brain is hardwired to survive. It will keep you emotionally and physically comfortable at all costs. That means it will accept roles in life to ensure you fit in, it will guard your ego through arrogance and self-protection, and it will pursue your personal desires and ambitions. It's all normal but doesn't lead to a fulfilling life. It's not true and real in human relationships.

Remember the Pixar movie *Wall-E*? The movie depicts a future human dystopia where everyone is shielded from the hard parts of being human. People's lives consist of facing a screen, consuming whatever they want, and never entering into hard human interactions. On the surface, everyone seems happy. But the reality is that they are craving something more meaningful, a pattern that isn't about themselves but is about the people and story around them.

So let's talk about how to make that kind of life happen.

PATTERN #4

HEALTHY OPERATIONS

The key to maintaining healthy thought, relationship, and ego patterns, is to commit to healthy operating patterns. Operating patterns are the systems, structures, and resource allocations you make with your limited time and energy. Like a stream of water flowing around the placement of rocks, your placement of time and resources will guide the flow of your thoughts, relationships, and priorities.

CHAPTER 12

MANAGING YOUR SCHEDULE AND ENERGY PATTERNS

Most of us spend too much time on what is urgent and not enough time on what is important.
– Stephen R. Covey

Review the schedules of some of the most admired people and you'll see a pattern emerge: intentional schedule and energy management.

Take Tim Ferriss, author of *The 4-Hour Workweek* and *Tools of Titans* (a book about the tactics, routines, and habits of world-class performers). He says repeatedly: "Winners have systems." By "system" he means diligently scheduling and protecting time on your calendar to do (or not do) a specific activity that leads to successful outcomes. Ferriss, for instance, doesn't take meetings or calls on Mondays and Fridays. And he carefully blocks time throughout the week to maintain patterns of sleep, study, meditation, healthy eating, and personal growth.[58, 59]

He knows what Daniel Pink revealed in his book *When: The Scientific Secrets of Perfect Timing*.[60] Human beings are freer, grow faster, and increase productivity when they carefully plan what priorities should be accomplished and when they are most important to execute. Don't just go through life succumbing to urges: demands from others, deadlines, distractions, and the constant flow of messages coming through your phone and inbox. Establish a pattern that reflects your priorities and gives you the energy you need to be your best self.

For years, I've experimented with various schedule patterns that keep me focused on my goals, and I've observed the scheduling patterns of people in many careers and parts of the world who lead a life of low anxiety, strong relationships, and alignment with their values. Here are key patterns that consistently emerge:

1. **Quality Sleep.** Most learning and memory consolidation occurs during your deepest nightly sleep. Poor quality sleep literally robs you of mental and emotional growth, not just physical health. According to sleep scientists, deep sleep improves substantially when all screens (television, phone, laptop, etc.) are turned off at least thirty minutes before falling asleep.[61] The glow of devices activates parts of your brain that are more difficult to quiet. Additionally,

sleep experts say that nearly everyone should have at least seven hours a night on a regular basis to function properly. If you're not sleeping enough, you're not growing enough.

2. **Inner Work.** To maintain and develop healthy patterns that lead to a meaningful life, it's necessary to spend time understanding your thoughts, emotions, and values. Inner work provides perspective on what you're learning, feeling, and experiencing, while also solidifying priorities and desired patterns.

   The bulk of the research around daily physiological cycles indicates that the general population is most mentally vigilant in the morning.[62] That means morning is the time when most people are best able to fend off distractions. It's during this time, when you are most vigilant and things are typically quieter, that you should reflect, pray, meditate, or journal.

3. **Counseling.** Most people benefit greatly from talking through their thoughts and experiences. To do that, you need a good counselor, coach, therapist, or friend who will listen extremely well. Often it's most helpful to work with someone who isn't part of your family, social, or work life so that they can remain non-anxious and fully confidential about what you're saying. Also, it's important that they not try to impress you or "fix" you and are not afraid to get into uncomfortable emotional territory.

4. **Planning.** This includes life planning, career planning, goal setting, and coordination for the week. Many people find it's important to schedule time—whether it be an annual retreat or a weekly calendar review—to clarify what's most important, how it will be executed, who will do what, and what needs to be prepared. Just make it a recurring meeting on your calendar.

5. **Body Care.** The one place you can never leave until you die is your body. So wouldn't you want to make that a healthy place? In fact, wouldn't you even want to see what it was capable of? Take care of it by setting patterns around healthy food purchases and preparation. Understand what food you should consume and when. Many people, for example, have experienced the benefits of only eating between 12:00 p.m. and 8:00 p.m., allowing their body to recover and remove unwanted calories and toxins.[63] Also, exercise, massage, physical therapy, and medicinal/herbal therapies all support a body so it can sustain and support a flourishing life over time. Understand your body and what it needs.

6. **Learning.** Meaningful patterns almost invariably include learning, regardless of your age. When you're in school, this is pretty easy. But even then, you can learn about current events and trends, learn new skills, and learn more about how the world works. Never in the history of the world have we had fewer excuses for not learning. News, books, and subject matter experts are literally at our fingertips with a decent internet connection.

7. **Connecting.** As we've discussed, relationships require intentionality. This might mean scheduling time for the people who matter to you. To thrive, you have to schedule your priorities. If your roommate from university is a priority, schedule time to talk to her on the phone every month. If your community is a priority, make time to show up.

8. **Work and Service.** And, of course, it's important to do work that creates value for others, whether you're 12 or 92. Maybe it's with your hands or perhaps with your mind. It might be paid or it might be volunteer. You may punch the time clock and wear a name tag, or you might be able to do your work from your home computer. Whether it's physical work or mental work, you can create value for someone. Set a pattern that ensures you're doing it well.

Consistent schedule and energy patterns do not make you a mundane or rigid person. They make you a consistent person. And being consistent raises the probability that you'll do the things that will make you the person you want to be.

You May Be Boring and You Might Disappoint People

James Clear says it this way: "The only way to become excellent is to be endlessly fascinated by doing the same thing over and over. You have to fall in love with boredom."[64]

Regardless of which scheduling patterns work best for you, maintaining an intentional schedule that promotes healthy patterns will require you to disappoint people. People will want to do things with you that hold you back or foster unproductive patterns. For instance, they may want you to stay out late, when you know your healthy patterns require more sleep. Or they may want you to do things that drain you and that you don't find restful.

People need rest, which is different from sleep. Allow yourself to recover and refill your inner tank. Take time "off" to remember who you are, who you aren't, and what's important. Establish screen time limits, social limits, and chemical (sugar, alcohol, caffeine) limits, as all of these (often good) things can exhaust you. They may provide immediate "highs" or generate peer approval but flame out fast like newspaper on a fire. Growing beyond patterns that aren't working for you requires strong, sustainable energy, not quick fixes.

There are costs and benefits to choices like these, and we need to consciously evaluate them, rather than going into autopilot and allowing our emotions and relationships to decide our actions.

Where could you be more intentional about productive schedule and energy patterns?

CHAPTER 13
PATTERNS OF TRANSPARENCY

Long-term relationships and life in a community of considerable duration may be essential if we are not to lose ourselves, if we are to be able to recollect ourselves. They may be essential to the human coherence of our lives, a coherence which is not found from looking into the faces of those who relieve us because we can see they know nothing of us when we were less than ourselves, but from looking into the faces of those who relieve us because they reflect our history in their faces, faces which we can look into finally without anger or shame, and which look back at us with love.
– Robert Kegan, *The Evolving Self*

Fifteen years ago, a dear friend of mine, older and wiser than me, asked whether I'd like to study a book with him and some other men. I suppose you'd call it a book club. He asked me to find the other men and he'd facilitate the discussions. There ended up being about five of us at a coffee shop.

The discussions weren't usually memorable or earth-shattering. We just kept meeting for an hour each week. Once the first book was completed, we selected another book. And on it went in the background of life, until one of the guys lost his job. He cried as he told us about the embarrassment he felt. "I trust you guys. Please keep it between us." No one tried to fix him or rescue him by offering quick, cheap solutions or platitudes. We just let him let his guard down.

Guys continued bringing things up, prompted by the environment of trust and the commitment of meeting regularly. Marriage conflict, miscarriages, depression, and the death of loved ones. Addiction, temptation, and anxiety. It all came up. Not every week, of course. Some weeks were mundane. Many weeks you could feel us reverting back to the societal expectations assumed by a group of men—act tough, solve problems, look successful. Guys would drop out of the group, maybe because of those societal norms or because they were busy or because they'd found another outlet like this.

But more guys joined than left. And guys kept coming. "I heard about your group," they'd say. You'd see their wives around town, and the women would pull you aside and whisper, "Thank you. This has been so good for him."

Some of the value may be a result of how countercultural it is for men to be vulnerable and to grow emotionally. Perhaps it's because guys receive a message from society that they are just supposed to plug into their career, be helpful at home, be ready to talk sports, and keep it all together. It can suffocate the soul. It's not just a guy thing. Society tells us all to hold it together and look strong.

The other reason why it's valuable is because it's a committed pattern.

Our group isn't alone. Alcoholics Anonymous is another great example of a consistent place where you see hardened adults (some criminals) open up vulnerably about themselves. Many of them experience tremendous freedom through their practice of vulnerability.

Showing your emotions doesn't necessarily mean you have to get emotional. Even the most stoic, reserved person can give voice to their emotions. In fact, expressing yourself emotionally can sometimes make it more difficult for others to understand your emotions. Vulnerability is about describing your emotions more than it's about acting emotionally.

In many parts of the world, there is a trend toward less authentic, committed community, and to greater loneliness.

A 2019 study by YouGov found that one in five millennials say that they have no friends, and three in ten millennials say that they always or often feel lonely, regardless of gender.[65] That makes them the least intimately connected generation. A 2018 US survey by health insurer Cigna, using one of the best-known tools for measuring loneliness, the UCLA Loneliness Scale, found that 54% of the 20,000 adults surveyed said that they always or sometimes feel that no one knows them well. And two in five felt like "they lack companionship," that their "relationships aren't meaningful," and that they "are isolated from others."[66] A 2014 study in the UK by Relate, a relationship support organization, reported that 42% of people have no friends at work. And 9% of the entire UK doesn't have a single close friend. That's about 4.7 million people.[67]

If you want to develop meaningful patterns, it's essential to find a consistent place where you can be transparent about your true self. It's by letting your guard down that self-awareness leads to new patterns, suffering builds strength, and clarity yields better choices. That may happen in a group of people, with a counselor or a friend, or through other channels like writing.

Scott Stossel decided in 2014, after years of a successful career as the national editor for *The Atlantic* magazine, that he wanted to be more transparent with his readers. He opened himself up to others in a big way by writing the *New York Times* bestseller *My Age of Anxiety: Fear, Hope, Dread, and the Search for Peace of Mind*. In it, he discusses in candid detail his struggles with anxiety. "To some people," he wrote, "I may seem calm. But if you could peer beneath the surface, you would see that I'm like a duck—paddling, paddling, paddling."[68]

He allowed himself to be seen by others for all of who he is, not just the polished, strong resume and social media persona. He did what Dr. Brené Brown describes so well in her book *Rising Strong*:

"Vulnerability is not winning or losing; it's having the courage to show up and be seen when we have no control over the outcome. Vulnerability is not weakness; it's our greatest measure of courage."[69]

Another example of committing to transparency through writing was the article Susan Borman wrote that was published in newspapers across the US in 1965 after she stood with her sons and watched her husband Frank shoot into orbit around the earth in Gemini 7. Susan wrote in response to some of the negative reactions she'd gotten from people, including at NASA, about how visibly scared she had been during the launch and flight. Her words and story can be found in Rocket Men, by Robert Kurson:

"These past weeks I had worn my feelings on my sleeve. Some said they were pleased to see an astronaut's wife willing to admit she was scared. Others, including some people in the space program, were critical because I failed to maintain the traditional stiff upper lip.... At one time, such criticism would have cut me deeply. But...I have come to realize you can't be all things to all people. So I decided not to pretend and not to try to hide my feelings—I decided to be myself."[70]

Leaders Need to Be Vulnerable

Do you sometimes struggle to give yourself full expression? To admit your attachments and insecurities? To speak your truth? To reveal who you really are?

It's very difficult, especially if people look to you for leadership or strength. You may not want to let people down or be perceived as weak. Consider the example of Lindsey Vonn, the most decorated female downhill skier of all time. She spent her entire childhood and adult years looking strong on ski runs and in front of the cameras. Then, nearly a year after retiring, and still fresh from the ego boost and adrenaline that comes from competing, she agreed to be the subject of an HBO documentary: *Lindsey Vonn, The Final Season*.

You'd expect a documentary about a champion to show her as polished and her life as epic. Instead, she honestly reveals her family challenges growing up, the need to find her identity in skiing because she couldn't find it elsewhere, her painful physical deterioration as she aged, and the emotional darkness of loss and broken relationships. Ironically, it caused most fans to admire her so much more than had the movie simply been about her triumphs. It was authentic.

It's not always easy for people to share thoughts like *I messed up* or *I'm really nervous*. But a leader or someone who's achieved success, who serves as a model, can make it safe to be vulnerable through their own example.

For his book *The Culture Code*, author Daniel Coyle researched teams with extraordinary cultures across multiple disciplines, including business, sports, entertainment, military, and education. One of his key revelations: make sure the leader is transparent first and often.

"Group cooperation is created by small, frequently repeated moments of vulnerability," he explains. "Of these, none carries more power than the moment when a leader signals vulnerability."[71] It's paramount for people to know that it's safe to tell the truth here.

You might be thinking, that works for Lindsey Vonn as an athlete, but it wouldn't work in a boardroom or a high-stakes business meeting.

Before you write off that level of exposure, imagine visiting a board meeting with Megan Tamte, whom we met in chapter 7. There you'll find savvy investors and business minds like Gordon Segal, co-founder and former chairman and CEO of Crate & Barrel. Yet, she's been known to admit to the board when she's nervous about discussing certain topics or delivering certain types of presentations that are outside her comfort zone. She shows up with honesty and goes for it anyway.

"I could keep my insecurities to myself, but instead I do it imperfectly. People love that," she recently told me. "When I'm in awkward, uncomfortable moments, I hear Brené Brown saying, 'Just show up and tell your story.'"

How do you develop a pattern to show up as you *really are*?

Know *who* you are and what you *really* value. Then the attachments to approval, success, and reputation will start to fade away.

Ironically, as Megan shows us, when you do this, greater trust and stronger relationships will come your way. If vulnerability is appropriate and communicated with the intent to simply be honest, it builds mutual appreciation.

Consider taking this assessment to better understand your transparency patterns in various areas. Indicate your score for each item accordingly:

1. Strongly disagree, 2. Somewhat disagree, 3. Unsure, 4. Somewhat agree, 5. Strongly agree.

#	Question	Item Score
Awareness		
1	I put myself in situations where others can give me honest feedback.	
2	I regularly think about the factors that are impacting trust in my relationships with others.	
3	I set aside time every day to think about how I'm feeling.	
4	I recognize symptoms (fatigue, anger, impatience, hunger, loneliness, etc.) of emotional depletion inside myself.	
	Section Total	
Environment		
5	I proactively talk about my feelings with my closest relationships.	
6	I can name three people with whom I can share anything about myself.	
7	I regularly meet with people where I talk about my feelings.	
8	I have a safe place to discuss my problems.	
	Section Total	
Mindset		
9	I see it as personal victory when I'm able to authentically share my feelings.	
10	I'm comfortable showing less socially normative emotions like sadness in front of people I trust.	
11	I view my ideal self as someone that can talk openly about my feelings.	
12	I value time spent talking about hard things with other people.	
	Section Total	
Communication		
13	I can clearly explain how I'm feeling to others.	
14	I know when to stop talking so that others can remain engaged in listening.	
15	I tell others about my emotions (how I'm feeling) beyond just telling them about circumstances (what's happening).	
16	I listen and ask questions when someone is sharing with me.	
	Section Total	
Response		
17	I honor the confidentiality expectations of others.	
18	I can listen to someone share their struggles with me without feeling compelled to give advice or solve their problems.	
19	I am careful not to make judging comments or jokes at the expense of others.	
20	I resist the temptation to minimize what people say to me by talking about my own similar experiences.	
	Section Total	

Go to www.mattnorman.com/patterns *for up-to-date printable forms like this one along with electronic assessments.*

Total up your score for each section and consider which section(s) score lowest. Pick one of the items in that section to work on, ideally with the help of other people who can model, encourage, and support your transparency. Maybe it's a group like a book club. Perhaps it's through a work team or in your marriage. Even if you've tended to be a private person or lacking in emotion, you can make this work. In the next chapter, we'll continue discussing how everybody, regardless of their background, can grow beyond the patterns that aren't working.

CHAPTER 14
A PATTERN OF CONTINUOUS GROWTH

Change is inevitable. Growth is optional. – John Maxwell

I suppose there are seasons of life that prompt the most pattern changes. Maybe puberty, leaving home, early years of marriage, start of a career, and having children are the big pattern adjustment phases. Also, patterns often have to change due to chronic illness and loss, aging parents, a shift to retirement, or career transitions.

Then again, perhaps pattern changes depend even more on how hard the people around you are pushing you to grow. I'm certain there are people who don't grow that much in their thought patterns, relationship patterns, ego patterns, and operating patterns throughout their entire adult lives. It may be too painful to self-confront and change. "This is just how I am," you might say. "I've done my growing." "It's too late to change." And maybe the people around you adjust themselves to you. "That's just the way she is," they might say. "You can't change her."

Maybe you should be able to reach pattern change retirement, because changing patterns is hard work, especially as you age. Pattern retirement might allow you to watch the television channels that reinforce your thinking, read the books that entertain you, travel to places where you're comfortable, and spend time with people who don't challenge you. Life is hard enough without pushing yourself to keep growing.

And maybe that's reasonable.

It feels, though, like a tree that gives up on extending its branches. It wouldn't be reaching its full potential. It wouldn't fully *be* what it means to be a *tree*. While trees eventually stop getting taller, they grow more actively as they age. It's the oldest trees that grow the most each year in width and take in the most carbon dioxide. They do far more work than younger trees. It's the pattern that trees follow.

Wouldn't it be bold and beautiful to be like an old tree, growing faster with age?

Countless people have demonstrated the ability to learn and grow in profound ways through older age, whether it's learning to play an instrument, becoming a marathon runner, or repairing broken relationships. It's never too late to change.[72]

Regardless of your age, having a growth mindset can have significant benefits. For instance, researchers at the University of Toronto made an important, though perhaps intuitive, discovery about the importance of a growth mindset in older adults. They assessed adults with an average age of 69 on their theories about growth and how old they felt. They also reported their perceptions of various positive behaviors such as sleep, diet, fitness, and seeking help. Not surprisingly, adults that believe their patterns are still very changeable felt younger and were more likely to engage in healthy behaviors.[73] The takeaway: never say "I'm just this way, and I'm too old or stuck to change."

You're also never too young to discover more productive patterns. Fred Rogers knew that better than most. The creator of *Mister Rogers' Neighborhood* wrote and edited all 895 episodes, played the piano, sang for most of the songs, and produced and approved every detail of the program because he believed so strongly that kids should develop healthy thought and relationship patterns. Patterns form early with children, and Rogers believed that their thought and relationship patterns "are mentionable and manageable." He saw children being bombarded with patterns of violence and superficiality on television and believed that "two men working out their feelings is much more dramatic than gunfire."

In 1969, Rogers testified before the US Senate Subcommittee on Communications to help persuade Congress to provide the $20 million in funding for public television (PBS) proposed by former President Lyndon Johnson, rather than the $9 million received under the Richard Nixon administration.[74] In that roughly seven-minute testimony, he succeeded in bringing the tough subcommittee chair Senator John Pastore of Rhode Island to tears as he read the lyrics to one of his songs, which talked about the feelings children have and how they might handle them.[75]

It was a powerful vision for healthy thinking, relationship, ego, and operating patterns. So powerful that congressional funding increased not to the $20 million target, but all the way to $22 million. And Nixon appointed Rogers as chair of the White House Conference on Children and Youth.

What's your mindset about growth? Do you operate with a continuous growth pattern? Or do you resign yourself and your children to accepting the patterns on television, at your country club, or in your retirement community?

If you're ready to grow, find someone who can hold you accountable and/or grow along with you. This might be your spouse or a trusted friend, co-worker, faith leader, or counselor. Whomever it is, establish a regular cadence (ideally every three months or less) to discuss pattern growth progress, increased self-awareness, and pattern growth goals. Refrain from making these interactions about fixing or judging one another. Instead, hold each other accountable to commitments and continuous growth. And be gracious and kind to one another, as pattern growth is often two steps forward and one step back.

CHAPTER 15

OPERATE AS A PATTERN DEVELOPER

The greatest leader is not necessarily the one who does the greatest things.
He is the one that gets the people to do the greatest things. – Ronald Reagan

What's the ultimate goal of improving your patterns? Certainly part of it is your own peace of mind and healthier relationships. That tends to lead to greater joy, trust, and support in life. As a result, you'll likely have a life filled with greater purpose and meaning, perhaps even longevity. People with stronger relationships and less stress tend to live longer.

Beyond all of these benefits, though, comes even greater impact: the opportunity to help others realize their own undiscovered greatness. As you parent, manage, coach, and lead, you'll be faced with countless opportunities to help others develop productive patterns. Your child may experience anxiety. Your husband might over-function as a leader, doing things for people that they can or should do for themselves. Perhaps your co-worker will have troubles expressing her own preferences or setting boundaries. You'll see these unhealthy patterns.

Regardless of your own patterns, you can probably do some active listening and offer some perspective when appropriate. Most effectively, you can lead by example! To see patterns and name them…that requires that you're willing to do some growing yourself.

If you've not done the inner work to develop healthier thought patterns, it will be difficult for you to empathize with the challenging thought patterns of someone else. If you haven't dealt with your own unhealthy relationship dynamics and ego patterns, you'll be a less safe person as you may unknowingly contribute to further dysfunction. And if you haven't established intentional systems for the way you operate your life, you'll likely be less available and vulnerable.

Conversely, as you help others grow, it will support your own maturity and development. It will increase your awareness of faulty patterns and your conviction to be a healthy person.

Helping others grow helps everyone grow. You don't need to be a therapist, counselor, minister, or coach. Decide to be a pattern developer.

Do you question whether you've earned the right to help others develop their patterns? Do you assume that your emotional growth would be too private or too unrelatable to others?

Consider the example of my friend Jay Bennett. As a corporate attorney and investor in Minneapolis, Jay spent the first half of his life climbing ladders and making big things happen. Then he had what he calls his "halftime moment" in reference to Bob Buford's book *Halftime: Moving from Success to Significance*.[76]

Due to a rare virus, he suddenly lost the ability to speak. You can imagine the limitations that would place on a lawyer.

Rather than become bitter, he got better. This tragic health condition made him realize that he had work to do in his thought patterns, relationship patterns, operating patterns, and especially his ego patterns. He became humbler; he more clearly defined his values and priorities apart from the demands of others; he became more transparent and spent significant time in quiet and solitude, improving relationships and increasing knowledge of himself. He began operating his life in much more alignment with what mattered most.

As a result of these changes, he made the decision to help others to grow the way he had. Pivoting from corporate law, he became a leader in a national nonprofit that helps people develop patterns of generosity. Additionally, he became a board member of Bob Buford's Halftime Institute in Dallas, where he counsels people on moving from success to significance.

I can personally attest that Jay lives for helping others based on the growth he himself has experienced. Countless times, he's listened and counseled my wife and me. (His voice has returned.) And he's often called upon to present the keynote address to top business leaders in our community.

He leveraged his own pattern growth to become a pattern developer for others.

Don't wait for your halftime moment. Don't wait for a crisis. Just assess your patterns and commit to growth in yourself and those around you.

CONCLUSION

That's the purpose of this book: to help you lead a more meaningful life, contribute to society in greater ways, and be of more value to others. It all comes down to your patterns. Consider your recurring tendencies in how you think, relate, prioritize yourself, and operate your life. Which patterns are working and which are leading you away from a more meaningful life and achieving your goals? Apply the ideas in this book to change your patterns so you can live your best life.

• • • • • • • • • • • • • • • • • •

One final note. I've mentioned throughout this book that I'm a person of faith. It's my faith, more than any "technique" or "strategy" that has contributed to my emotional growth and the growth I've seen in others.

In fact, it's through my faith that I've come to learn and believe that the point of life IS to grow.... Not to be comfortable or successful as the world might tell you, and the beauty of it is, everyone has access to this their entire life. Ironically, the more suffering one endures in life the more opportunity they typically find for growth.

Everyone has faith in something. When it comes to changing thought patterns, improving relationships, reducing ego, and operating a fuller, more authentic life, people put their faith in something...science, human progress, achievement, self-help gurus, or God, to name a few options. I'm not here to tell you where to put your faith. Just consider this. What you believe about the world and why you exist will invariably form your patterns. It will whisper verdicts about your identity and the point of suffering. It will be the filter through which you evaluate mistakes, challenges, and tensions.

There's no doubt that "religious leaders" and "religious systems" throughout history have had mixed success in helping people develop productive patterns. In some cases, they've contributed to people getting stuck in bad patterns. I'm not talking about that.

What I'm describing is faith in something that has the power to transform your patterns into patterns that change the world. It's the faith and pattern of Mother Theresa and Dr. Martin Luther King. That's the faith that fueled the Missionaries of Charity, the American civil rights movement, and Alcoholics Anonymous. It's a faith based on acceptance of your limits, and love of everyone as they are. That's the faith that continues to transform my life and the lives of so many others I've seen.

Wherever you put your faith, I hope it contributes to your flourishing patterns.

GRATITUDE

Thanks so much for purchasing this book. It's my sincere goal to provide insight and strategies to help readers understand their individual patterns and enhance their lives.

Readers look forward to reviews, and honest thoughtful feedback helps others find this book. Please take just a moment of your time to share your feedback on Amazon, or wherever you found this title. It would mean the world to me. Thanks again for reading and for any thoughts you share.

ABOUT THE AUTHOR

Matt Norman coaches and advises executives on how to build great people and culture.

He is President & CEO of Norman & Associates, which offers custom coaching and consulting in the areas of talent strategy, personal effectiveness, planning, and goal alignment.

Norman & Associates also provides Dale Carnegie cohort-style action learning programs to help people improve how they communicate, lead, influence, and work together.

He hosts professional training courses on personal and organizational effectiveness and speaks at seminars and workshops throughout the country. You can learn more about these events and read Matt's articles at http://mattnorman.com.

ENDNOTES

1   Alice Schroeder, *The Snowball: Warren Buffett and the Busines of Life* (New York: Bantam, 2009).

2   https://money.cnn.com/2005/01/28/news/newsmakers/buffett/index.htm

3   Hannah Fry, *The Mathematics of Love: Patterns, Proofs, and the Search for the Ultimate Equation* (New York: Simon and Schuster, 2015).

4   https://www.simplypsychology.org/classical-conditioning.html

5   https://www.nytimes.com/2020/02/17/well/eat/the-benefits-of-intermittent-fasting.html

6   https://www.imdb.com/title/tt1504320/

7   https://www.notablebiographies.com/We-Z/Winfrey-Oprah.html

8   https://www.gottman.com/blog/seriously-whats-point-marriage-growth/

9   David Bakan, *The duality of human existence: Isolation and communion in Western man* (Boston: Beacon Press, 1966.)

10   Robert Kegan, *The Evolving Self: Problem and Process in Human Development* (Cambridge, MA: Harvard University Press, 1982).

11   Carol S. Dweck, *Mindset: The New Psychology of Success* (New York: Penguin Random House, 2007).

12   https://onlinelibrary.wiley.com/doi/abs/10.1046/j.1460-9568.2003.02675.x

13   https://www.cnbc.com/2018/03/22/how-scott-harrison-founded-charity-water.html

14   https://smile.amazon.com/Thirst-Story-Redemption-Compassion-Mission/dp/1524762849/ref=sr_1_1?dchild=1&keywords=thirst&qid=1592851623&s=books&sr=1-1

15   https://people.com/sports/tiger-woods-sex-scandal-thinks-about-every-day/

16   https://www.who.int/mental_health/world-mental-health-day/2017/en/

17   https://www.wsj.com/articles/the-latest-perk-for-stressed-out-office-workers-therapy-comes-to-you-11580486984?mod=searchresults&page=1&pos=2

18   https://www.theplayerstribune.com/en-us/articles/rick-ankiel-letter-to-my-younger-self-cardinals

19   https://www.nytimes.com/2015/08/31/sports/tennis/before-saying-farewell-at-us-open-mardy-fish-intends-to-stay-for-a-while.html

20   https://www.usatoday.com/story/sports/2017/08/30/michael-phelps-brandon-marshall-mental-health-battles-royce-white-jerry-west/596857001/

21   https://www.ncbi.nlm.nih.gov/pmc/articles/PMC5177451/

22   Dennis Greenberger and Christine A Padesky, *Mind Over Mood, Second Edition: Change How You Feel by Changing the Way You Think* (New York: Guilford Press, 2015).

23   http://changingminds.org/explanations/perception/attention/what_attention.htm

24   https://www.bbc.com/future/article/20160928-how-anxiety-warps-your-perception

25   Alex Hutchinson, *Endure: Mind, Body, and the Curiously Elastic Limits of Human Performance* (New York: William Morrow, 2018).

26   https://vimeo.com/261201087

27   https://www.simplypsychology.org/carl-rogers.html

28   https://www.cnbc.com/2019/03/21/billionaire-warren-buffett-says-a-100-dollar-course-had-the-biggest-impact-on-his-success.html

29   Seth Godin, *Linchpin: Are You Indispensable?* (New York: Portfolio, 2011).

30   https://medium.com/@willkrieger/your-crucible-moments-35994634a312

31   https://www.youtube.com/watch?v=ZFWyseydTkQ

32   https://www.gottman.com/blog/attachment-differentiation-relationships-interview-ellyn-bader-ph-d/

33   https://www.gottman.com/blog/attachment-differentiation-relationships-interview-ellyn-bader-ph-d/

34   https://thebowencenter.org/theory/

35   https://thebowencenter.org/theory/

36   Stephen M. R. Covey, *The Speed of Trust: The One Thing That Changes Everything* (Salt Lake City, UT: FranklinCovey, 2008).

37   https://www.gottman.com/blog/the-four-horsemen-defensiveness/

38   https://www.simplypsychology.org/fundamental-attribution.html

39   https://ethicsunwrapped.utexas.edu/glossary/fundamental-attribution-error

40   https://www.amazon.com/Difficult-Conversations-audiobook/dp/B00005454M

41   https://www.cnvc.org/learn-nvc/what-is-nvc

42   Doris Kearns Goodwin, *Team of Rivals: The Political Genius of Abraham Lincoln* (New York: Simon & Schuster, 2005).

43   https://hbr.org/2018/09/curiosity

44   Veronica Roth, *Divergent* (New York: HarperCollins, 2011).

45   https://www.businessinsider.com/microsoft-hr-chief-kathleen-hogan-company-culture-change-satya-nadella-2019-8

46   http://thebowencenter.org/theory/eight-concepts/

47   http://www.nbcnews.com/id/35804710/ns/us_news-giving/t/uk-millionaire-move-mud-hut/#.XvJOY2hKhPZ

48   https://www.jimcollins.com/concepts/level-five-leadership.html

49   Dick Winters, *Beyond Band of Brothers: The War Memoirs of Major Dick Winters* (Toronto: Dutton Caliber, 2006).

50   https://journals.sagepub.com/doi/abs/10.1177/0149206315604187?mod=article_inline&

51   https://www.bbc.com/news/av/magazine-39490507/how-princess-diana-changed-attitudes-to-aids

52   Carlo Carretto, *Letters from the Desert* (New York: Orbis Books, 1982).

53   James Clear, *Atomic Habits: An Easy & Proven Way to Build Good Habits and Break Bad Ones* (New York: Penguin Random House, 2019).

54   Martin Buber, *I and Thou* (Chicago: Martino Publishing, 2010).

55   https://www.youtube.com/watch?v=MkFQHScyti0

56   Bryan E. Robinson, *Chained to the Desk (Third Edition): A Guidebook for Workaholics, Their Partners and Children, and the Clinicians Who Treat Them* (New York: NYU Press, 2014).

57   https://www.ajc.com/news/the-renegade-preacher/EI73LYvEX1yM34nAD2sXTJ/

58   Timothy Ferris, *The 4-Hour Workweek: Escape 9-5, Live Anywhere, and Join the New Rich* (New York: Harmony, 2009).

59   Tim Ferris, *Tools of Titans: The Tactics, Routines, and Habits of Billionaires, Icons, and World-Class Performers* (Boston: Houghton Mifflin Harcourt, 2016).

60   Daniel H. Pink, *When: The Scientific Secrets of Perfect Timing* (New York: Riverhead Books, 2018).

61   https://med.stanford.edu/sleepdivision/research.html

62   Daniel H. Pink, *When: The Scientific Secrets of Perfect Timing* (New York: Riverhead Books, 2018).

63   https://www.nia.nih.gov/news/research-intermittent-fasting-shows-health-benefits

64   James Clear, *Atomic Habits: An Easy & Proven Way to Build Good Habits and Break Bad Ones* (New York: Penguin Random House, 2019).

65   https://today.yougov.com/topics/lifestyle/articles-reports/2019/07/30/loneliness-friendship-new-friends-poll-survey

66   https://www.multivu.com/players/English/8294451-cigna-us-loneliness-survey/

67   https://www.theguardian.com/lifeandstyle/2014/aug/12/one-in-ten-people-have-no-close-friends-relate

68   Scott Stossel, *My Age of Anxiety: Fear, Hope, Dread, and the Search for Peace of Mind* (New York: Vintage, 2015).

69   Brené Brown, *Rising Strong: The Reckoning. The Rumble. The Revolution* (New York: Random House, 2015).

70   Robert Kurson, *Rocket Men: The Daring Odyssey of Apollo 8 and the Astronauts Who Made Man's First Journey to the Moon* (New York: Random House, 2018).

71   Daniel Coyle, *The Culture Code: The Secrets of Highly Successful Groups* (New York, Bantam, 2018).

72   https://blogs.scientificamerican.com/observations/think-youre-too-old-to-learn-new-tricks/

73   https://www.ncbi.nlm.nih.gov/pmc/articles/PMC6230032/

74   https://www.youtube.com/watch?v=fKy7ljRr0AA

75   https://www.youtube.com/watch?v=viqPDiH7M9A

76   Bob Buford, *Halftime: Moving from Success to Significance* (Grand Rapids, MI: Zondervan, 2015).

Made in the USA
Monee, IL
16 August 2021